A Chaucerian Puzzle
and other
Medieval Essays

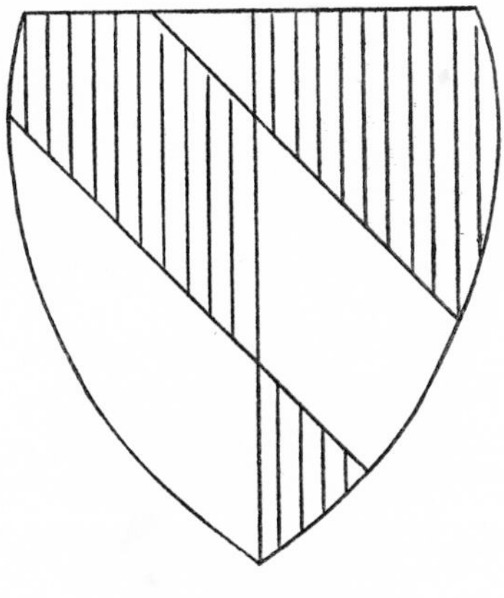

University of Miami Publications
in
English and American Literature.

Number V October, 1961.

A CHAUCERIAN PUZZLE
and other
MEDIEVAL ESSAYS

Edited by
Natalie Grimes Lawrence
Jack A. Reynolds

UNIVERSITY OF MIAMI PRESS
CORAL GABLES, FLORIDA
1961

Library of Congress Card Number: 61-17983

Printed in the United States of America

by

Rose Printing Company

Tallahassee, Miami, Jacksonville, St. Augustine

Introduction

Whether you and I care to admit it publicly, the simple fact remains that we are the grandchildren and heirs of the Middle Ages, whether we date that elastic period traditionally from 500 to 1500 A.D. or (as I personally prefer) beginning in the Mediterranean area with the labors of St. Paul and ending in the British Isles with the first great impact of the Industrial Revolution. Viewed this way, the Renaissance becomes its proper flowering and the Reformation its self-voiced protest and partial repudiation.

The heritage is a mixed one, and I leave it to the reader to evaluate its specific items. Some of them began as mere acorns, but the subsequent behavior of acorns is proverbial. Every school child knows the Middle Ages gave us the military use of gun powder; but, quite simultaneously, the personally distinguishing crest on the knight's helmet. They gave us too the tales of romantic love, perhaps the very concept itself. Less well known is the stirrup; this curious footgear may have been the deciding factor in turning back the Asiatic hordes. The book you are reading is a codex (as distinguished from a scroll); it comes from the same period, and so do the upper and lower case letters in which it is printed. So does printing itself.

The theology of the Middle Ages is still the reasonably orthodox theology of today, its cassock generally exchanged for a cutty sark. While all modern heresies on close inspection appear no less heretical, they reveal themselves as something less than modern.

The most stimulating theatrical performance and the most soporific soap-opera had their beginning within the altar rail of an unknown French church in the ninth century.

But, of course, the modern world has its scientist in his white coat. He didn't appear *sui generis;* his great-grandfather wore a conical cap. It is self-gratifying to laugh at those old fools who believed that we could, by changing the atomic structure of base metals, remake them to our heart's desire. But not many of us may live to laugh out of the other side of the mouth.

I suppose we have lost much of the old heritage (some good, some bad); and I suppose we have acquired much of a new heritage (again of mixed values). As a modern man with a reasonable degree of respect for my own age, I should not like the task of casting the accounts.

J. A. Reynolds
Coral Gables, Florida
August 1961

Contents

Hazel Sullivan

A Chaucerian Puzzle

Part I

The Puzzle

T*here are fewer published* speculations concerning the *Shipman's Tale* than occur with regard to other *Canterbury Tales.* The few commentaries that have accumulated compensate for their paucity by a singularly insistent repetition of a guess which seems wilder, yet more widely accepted, than most literary speculations. This is the assumption that the Tale was originally meant for the Wife of Bath instead of for the Shipman. The basis for the theory is the five feminine pronouns in the Tale's beginning. They occur in a first-person generalization which interrupts the third-person setting of the story's scene and the introduction of its three main characters. There is a far simpler and more logical possible explanation for the pronouns and other misfit facets of the passage than the one generally proposed and accepted, yet this simpler solution seems to have been overlooked.

With the interrupting interpolation in italics for clarity and emphasis, to set it out from the story's four lines of character-presenting introduction, the beginning of the Tale reads:[1]

Page *Line*

156

A marchant whilom dwelled at Seint-Denys
That riche was, for which men helde hym wys.
A wyf he hadde of excellent beautee
And compaignable and revelous was she.
Which is a thyng that causeth more dispence
Than worth is al the chiere and reverence
That men hem doon at festes and at daunces.
Swiche salutaciouns and contenaunces
Passen as dooth a shadwe upon the wal;
But wo is hym that payen moot for all!
The sely housbonde, algate he moot paye,
He moot us clothe, and he moot us arraye,
Al for his owene worshipe richely.
In which array we daunce jolily.
And if that he noght may, par aventure
Or ellis list no swich dispence endure
But thynketh it is wasted and ylost
Thanne moot another payen for oure cost.
Or lene us gold, and that is perilous.
This noble marchant heeld a worthy hous . . .

Reading the *Canterbury Tales* carefully, with attention to the ways in which Chaucer habitually prepares for his interpolations and proceeds later to make transitions back to the story thread, reveals that no matter for whom lines 5-19 were intended, they not only do not fit the story opening, but are apparently misarranged within the passage itself.

1. There is a four-line gap in the antecedent clause, "algate he moot paye," line eleven, and its dependent conditional clause in line fifteen, "And if that he noght may, par aventure."

2. There is a person, number and gender shift without a transition in lines 12-14.

3. There is a style shift from narration to philosophizing without a transitional bridge.

4. There is no transition from the interrupting passage, lines 5-19, to the resumed story thread in line twenty.

5. There is a separation of seventeen lines between the mentions of the Merchant and his wife in the Tale's first three lines and the mention of him again in line twenty. There are twenty-one lines separating the introduction of the Merchant and his wife and the first mention of the Monk. This delay in completing the orienting of the plot factors is caused solely by the disrupting insertions of misfit commentary matter.

Since the passage is startling and disrupts the important start of the story where the author is introducing the reader into the basic circumstances of the plot, where would it fit in better?

It fits smoothly and logically into the dialogue of the Wife of St. Denys when she talks in her garden with the Monk. It provides convincing extra points of argument while she is persuading the Monk to lend her money, and it is entirely in keeping with her talent for persuasion by means of argument. Also, line 13, "Al for his owene worshipe richely," is a part of her philosophy as expressed in her dialogue in line 179, "For his honour, myself for to arraye."

The only sacrifice called for in shifting the troublesome passage from the story's opening on Page 156 to the dialogue on Pages 157-158 is the loss of line 19: "Or lene us gold and that is perilous."[2]

But besides the likelihood that Chaucer would have written, "and that *were* perilous," since, where the subjunctive is indicated he tends to use it, there is other evidence that this line may have been supplied spuriously and in the wrong place, for rhyme's sake. A more logical line with no rhyme-split between passages of the story may well have followed line twenty as Chaucer wrote the Tale.

Here is the dialogue passage with the disputed lines *rearranged, inserted* and italicized for clarity:

Line

158: "My deere love," quod she, "O my daun John
Ful lief were me this conseil for to hyde.
160: But out it moot, I may namoore abyde.
Myn housbonde is to me the worste man
That evere was sith that the world bigan.
But sith I am a wyf, it sit nat me
165: To tellen no wight of oure privatee,
Neither abedde, ne in noon oother place;
God shilde I sholde it tellen for his grace!
A wyfe ne shal nat seyn of hir housbonde
But al honour, as I kan understonde;
Save unto yow thus much I tellen shal,
170: As helpe me God, he is noght worth at al
In no degree the value of a flye.
172: But yet me greveth moost his nygardye.
11: *The sely housbonde, algate he moot paye,*
12: *He moot us clothe, and he moot us arraye,*
13: *Al for his owene worship richely,*
14: *In which arraye we daunce jolily.*
5: *Which is a thyng that causeth more dispence*
6: *Than worth is al the chiere and reverence*
7: *That men hem doon at festes and at daunces.*
8: *Swich salutaciouns and contenaunces*
9: *Passen as dooth a shadwe upon the wal;*
10: *But wo is hym that payen moot for al!*
15: *And if that he noght may, par aventure,*
16: *Or ellis list no swich dispence endure,*
17: *But thynketh it is wasted and ylost*
18: *Than moot another payen for oure cost.*
173: And wel ye woot that women naturally
174: Desiren thynges sixe as well as I:
175: They wolde that hir housbondes sholde be
Hardy, and wise, and riche, and thereto free,
And buxom unto his wyf, and fresshe abedde.

But by that ilke Lord that for us bledde,
For his honour, myself to arraye,
A Sonday next I moste nedes paye
An hundred frankes, or ellis I am lorn.
Yet were me levere that I were unborn
Than we were doon a sclaundre or vileyne;
And if myn housbonde eek it myghte espye
I nere but lost; and therefore I yow preye,
Lene me this somme, or ellis moot I deye.
Daun John, I seye, lene me thise hundred
 frankes.
Pardee, I wol nat faille yow my thankes,
If that yow list to doon that I yow praye.
For at a certyn day I wol yow paye,
And doon to yow what plesance and service
That I may doon, right as yow list devise.
And but I do, God take on me vengeance
As foul as evere hadde Genylon of France.[3]

It will be noted that now the syntax between the verbal phrase, "payen moot for al!" and its dependent conditional related clause, "and if that he noght may, par aventure," is close instead of separated by four lines of extraneous text.

The sacrificed split-rhyme line "Or lene us gold, and that is perilous," is unconvincing for a woman to speak, yet it is obvious from the feminine pronouns that the disputed passage was written for a woman. Therefore, this line sounds like a rather poor convenience line contributed by a scribe doing a careless job of patching to create an end-rhyme for "This noble merchaunt heeld a worthy hous."

There is also evidence that it may be misplaced. This is shown by the odd use of "For" in the line following "hous," which seems definitely a misfit as the passage stands:

Page *Line*

156 20: This noble marchaunt heeld a worthy
 hous,

For which he had alday so greet repair
For his largesse, and for his wyf was
fair,
That wonder is; but herkneth to my tale.
Amonges alle his gestes, grete and smale,
Ther was a monk, a fair man and a boold - -
I trowe a thritty wynter he was oold - -
That evere in oon was drawynge to that
place.

Surely the merchant's guests would repair "to" his house, not "for" it. If a different end-rhyme instead of "perilous" had *followed* "hous," describing the merchant's food, wine or hospitality, then the word "for" in the line "For which he had alday so greet repair," would fit perfectly. At best, "perilous-hous" is a rhyme split between passages, without transition.

Chaucer and split rhymes are not strangers, but in general it is apparent that Chaucer himself tends to avoid them. Where they occur there is usually some circumstance indicating tampering or patching with end-rhyme lines put in by someone less talented and conscientious than Chaucer. Eleanor Prescott Hammond quotes George Frederick Nott, from his "Dissertation on the State of English Poetry Before the Sixteenth Century" as listing the establishment of the practice of changing the line with the couplet as one of the four improvements made by Geoffrey Chaucer in the art of versification.[4]

That Chaucer was afraid his work would be tampered with after his death, or that copyists' carelessness might change his meaning, is proved in his apostrophe beginning, "Go litel bok, litel myn tragedye," inserted into the end of the Fifth Book of *Troilus and Criseyde:*

And for there is so gret diversite
In Englissh and in writyng of oure tonge,
So prey I God that non myswrite the,
Ne the mysmetre for defaute of tonge.
And red whereso thow be, or elles songe
That thow be understonde, God I biseche.[5]

That Chaucer's fear of manuscript-altering was justified is shown by evidence that while alive he was hard put to keep his scribes from changing his lines and causing him trouble in re-editing "fair" copies. In "Wordes unto Adam, His owne Scriven" he pleads:

> Adam scriveyn, if ever it the bifalle
> Boece or Troylus for to wryten newe,
> Under thy long lokkes thou most have the
>   scalle,
> But after my makyng thou wryte more trewe;
> So ofte a-daye I mot thy werk renewe.
> It is to correcte and eek to rubbe and scrape;
> And al is thorough thy negligence and rape.[6]

Now, how does the beginning of the *Shipman's Tale* read without the puzzling and disrupting passage?

> 1: A marchant whilom dwelled at Saint-Denys
> That riche was, for which men helde hym wys.
> A wyf he hadde of excellent beautee;
> And compaignable and revelous was she.
> 20: This noble marchaunt heeld a worthy hous[7]
> For which he hadde alday so greet repair,
> For his largesse, and for his wyf was fair
> That wonder is; but herkneth to my tale.
> Amonges alle his gestes, grete and smale,
> 25: There was a monk, a fair man and a boold - -
> I trow a thritty wynter he was oold - -
> That evere in oon was drawynge to that place.

Again it will be noted, relating is much closer. Only the couplet mentioning the wife separates the two mentions of the Merchant. Only one line intervenes between the description of the wife and the introduction of the Monk, completing the triangle quickly. The story opening is compact, revealing the economy and fidelity, in giving his readers quick and clear orientation, which is characteristic of Chaucer. The passage's only blemishes are the missing rhyme line to follow "hous" and provide for the otherwise awkward use of "for" where "to" would seem to belong, plus the interrupted line marring all extant manuscripts in which its portion occurs: "That wonder is but herkneth to my tale."

This line, in modern editions, has had a semicolon inserted arbitrarily to try to mitigate the un-Chaucerian stopping of a thought in mid-center to interpolate a request for attention. Extant manuscripts of fifteenth-century scribes have no punctuation inside the lines. Chaucer has phrases similar to "That wonder is" but in other places where it occurs he completes the thought.

The incompleteness here indicates further that the *Shipman's Tale* was put together, jig-saw fashion, by some scribe whose copy was used as an arch-ancestor for all extant manuscripts of the story, and that a tear or burn had taken away a part of the line which Chaucer had begun with "That wonder is." Or that a scribe had divided the line as originally written between two pages of a folio, made an error on the second and cut it from the folio and lost it. Any of these mishaps could account at the same time for the separation of the beginning of the *Shipman's Tale* from other parts of the story, and, in several extant manuscripts, the beginning is missing altogether with no attempt to patch it in.

That the interpolation including the "sely housbonde" passage and the five lines preceding it was in two pieces and that these were erroneously transposed seems obvious from the improvement in syntax when the "sely housbonde" passage is placed first inside the dialogue of the Wife of St. Denys, letting lines 5-10 follow "In which array we daunce jolily."

It is easy to see in that case, how the patching scribe, faced with two separated bits of one sequence, with no quotation marks as a clue that it was meant to be dialogue, might be excused for placing them as he did, providing he was so careless as not to spot the drastic shift of style, the lack of transitions at the beginning and end of the interpolation, and the feminine plural pronouns. Knowing Chaucer's habit of close syntax and noting the chance to insert the lines containing "payen moot for al!" at line ten and "algate he moot paye" in line eleven, he might take this as a clue for putting the bits in the order in which they appear in all surviving manuscripts in which the *Shipman's Tale* is relatively complete. A careful inspection would have shown the serious lacks of even reasonably close syntax elsewhere, together with the complete lack of transitions. Inside the dialogue of the Wife of St. Denys not one of these faults mars the passage. Further indication of the jig-saw assembling of the Tale, which seems to show the insertion of a bit from some other story altogether, is shown in the three lines starting with line ninety-five:

> A mayde child cam in hire compaignye
> Which as hir list she may governe and gye
> For yet under the yerde was the mayde.[8]

This child is mentioned nowhere else in the *Shipman's Tale*. The wife and the Monk swear each other to secrecy, and she maligns her husband, stating that she would rather never have been born than be slandered. Before the oaths of secrecy and the kissing of the breviary she says she must die if the Monk refuses the loan. Yet this child who contributes nothing except incredulity is present at the interview. If she belonged in the story and were a bond servant, surely the wife would send her away. She is not a baby, but a minor "still under the yerde." Chaucer is notably economical, rarely introducing useless cast. There is no mention of the Merchant and his wife having children, or having additional guests.

The *Shipman's Tale* is classified consistently as a *fabliau* of the "Lover's Gift Regained" category. In no version of the "Lover's Gift Regained" stories cited by Dr. John Webster Spargo,[9] is a child included in the plot. The story line is triangular in casting except when a witness[10] or a messenger[11] is introduced by the "lover" to prove that the wife has accepted money or a pledge of merchandise and has "refused to return the pledge."

It is stated in Line 94 of the text that the Wife of St. Denys was in the habit of strolling in her garden and talking to the Monk: "And hym saleweth, as she hath doon ofte." This makes it still less credible that she would take along a child who would overhear their conservation, which she would rather die than have repeated. For these reasons it seems most unlikely that the lines concerning the maiden child were meant by Chaucer for this story. As frequently occurs when a questionable passage seems to have been inserted spuriously, this passage ends in half of a split rhyme.

Chaucer is conceded to have died in 1400. The length of his illness can only be surmised. Dr. Robinson reports in the biographical section to the Introduction of his text that Chaucer took a 53-year-lease on a house in the garden of Westminster Abbey on December 4, 1399. The last recorded payment of his annuity, renewed in 1399, was dated June 5, 1400. According to the date on his tomb in Westminster Abbey he died on October 25 of that same year.[12] These data are also given by Thomas Lounsbury with additional details.[13]

None of the extant manuscripts and fragments of the *Canterbury Tales* are conceded to be Chaucer originals. According to Manly and Rickert,[14] only four are judged to date between 1400 and 1410: Additional 4, Ellesmere, Hengwrt and Marthyr. The next earliest, Harley 4,7334, is attributed to 1410. Some of these could have been partially edited in early 1400 before Chaucer became too ill to collect his annuity, but his death four months later would seem to make this unlikely. There is no proof that any of the manuscripts date as early as the turn of the century.

There are 58 relatively complete *Canterbury Tales* manuscripts,[15] though all have some parts of some tales missing.

The *Shipman's Tale* is in all of the relatively complete manuscripts, according to Manly and Rickert, except

Harley 7333 and Helmingham, where it seems not to have appeared in the ancestor, and Harley 5, where the end of the manuscript is lost. Manly and Rickert say:

> Gaps caused by the loss of leaves are as follows: Ad 2, E. 1014; B 1491; Ad 3, B 1608-70; Dd 1584-1663; En^2, lines 7-12 of the spurious link and lines 1191-1262; 1339-1414; Gg, 1191-1252; 1563-1747; Holkham, 1305-1610; and Phillippe, 1368-1446.

These data are useful merely to show the carelessness of scribes and the loss of parts of Chaucer manuscripts, because the mutilation and patching of the *Shipman's Tale* would have had to occur prior to extant copies, that is, in the hypothetical ancestor, since the awkward arrangement of the bothersome lines and their inconsistency is apparent, if the beginning of the Tale is present, in all extant *Shipman's Tale* manuscripts.

The Bodley 686 manuscript, Manly and Rickert say, has the *Shipman's Tale* headed "Pardoner's" and they note: "Evidence of resumption of work after interruption, under different auspices. Contains many spurious lines and other errors in the *Canterbury Tales* portion, with the *Merchant's Tale* attributed to Lydgate."[16]

The same authorities in their definitive and exhaustive printing of all known Canterbury Tales manuscripts, (quoted in preceding paragraphs here) and sometimes called the "Chicago Collation," say:

> In A 1740-3840, Vc is from the same source as the later Vb and affiliated MSS . . .
>
> In a few other Tales c and d are together but undistinguishable: *Second Nun's Tale, Shipman's Tale, Priest's Tale* . . . Vc must have been badly damaged before any of its descendants were copied.[17]

In the Cambridge gg manuscript the beginning to Line 1252 is missing and in the Edgerton 2 the beginning is missing up to line 1262. (Line 1252 is "Er he to Brugges went in alle wys''[18] and line 1262 reads: ''And volatil as ay was his usage.'')[19] Both these omissions of the *Shipman's Tale* beginning include the questionable ''Which is a thyng'' and ''sely housbonde'' passages containing the misfit pronouns and the other evidences of patching: reversed arrangement, the fragmentary ''That wonder is'' line, and the apparently inserted-for-rhyme-convenience line, ''Or lene us gold and that is perilous.'' The need to write in a rhyme line would have been created artificially by the scrivener's inserting by mistake the passage-fragments belonging inside dialogue farther along in the story, into the narrative-opening of the tale.

Manly and Rickert point out that there are several tales which appear in one version only: ''The ReT, FrT, *Shipman's Tale,* Pr. T. and, doubtfully, a few others.''[20] These appear in one version in extant manuscripts, the authors say, ''in all but a few related MSS whose scribes became impatient and cut the text drastically.'' The assumption has been that this consistency of version implies that these consistent manuscripts exist ''in their original form,'' but surely it could as well imply that they happened to be copied from a single ancestor, which was, itself, a careless patched-up copy produced by a scrivener during Chaucer's illness or after his death.

Obviously Chaucer was justified in his feeling that his manuscripts would be mishandled. This would seem to make it still more unfair to charge him with such arrant carelessness as the change of the assignment of a whole story from a feminine narrator to a masculine speaker without taking the elementary precaution of glancing at the manuscript to make sure the arrangement remained as intended and that the pronouns, style and syntax would fit. It seems especially unjust in view of the many proofs, organic in his work, that Chaucer cared very much how his manuscripts read, and that he took great care for verisimilitude and fitness in assigning tale to relator.

Part II

The House Of Straw

H*ow, then, did the* increasingly positive statement that "Chaucer originally meant the *Shipman's Tale* for the Wife of Bath and forgot to change the feminine pronouns" gain its popularity?

It seems to have started with a mere tentative suggestion and to have grown from that weak straw foundation into a structure of statements made as didactically as if based on proven fact. The wider the reputation of the writer, and the less credit he gave to his suggesting source, the more his imitators failed to credit him and to expand his positively-voiced guess into more elaborate additions to the growing House of Straw.

Apparently Thomas Tyrwhitt made the first tentative suggestion, basing it on the feminine pronouns alone, without observing that the whole fifteen-line passage was misfit in other ways. In her revised edition of *Chaucer, a Bibliographical Manual,* Eleanor Prescott Hammond writes:

> It was first remarked by Thos. Tyrwhitt in his note on l. 12492 that the pronouns here 'would lead

> one to suspect that this tale was originally intended for a female character.' Bell, in his edition of 1854, 111:92, note, considers Tyrwhitt's suggestion 'scarcely credible.' Hertzberg, p. 643-4, is of the same opinion as Tyrwhitt; von Düring, 111:427-8, cites ten Brink as suggesting that this tale was once a woman's; von Düring adds, 'perhaps the Wife of Bath's though the matter is not fully decided and it may even be that Chaucer would allow himself the liberty of varying his pronouns in a Tale which presents now the views of one sex, now those of another.' Ten Brink himself, *Hist. Eng. Lit.:* 172 says the Tale was 'originally written for the Wife of Bath.''[21]

Illuminatingly significant points can be noted in the foregoing Hammond quotation. First, Tyrwhitt's guess was merely the suggestion of a suspicion. Ten Brink's *first* mention was described, by his follower, von Düring, as a "suggestion" also. But note how von Düring has added, very tentatively and with an alternate choice, that the story was "perhaps the Wife of Bath's, though the matter is not fully decided, and it may even be that Chaucer would allow himself the liberty," etc. Then see how ten Brink takes *that,* plus his own former mere suggestion, and makes of it a positive statement that the *Shipman's Tale* "was originally written for the Wife of Bath."

Already the House of Straw has grown from its original tentative suggestion to outright positive statement, with the Wife of Bath squeezing through an opening in the straw wall midway of the first story of the structure.

Other high-ranking Chaucer authorities slipped whole stories of straw in between the units of the growing structure. In 1894, the Rev. Walter W. Skeat, editor of the Oxford edition of Chaucer,[22] said of the *Shipman's Tale*:

> There is a curious difficulty in the opening lines of this Tale. The use of the words *us* (B 1202, 1209) *we* (1204), and *our* (1208),[23] certainly show that, in the first instance, this Tale was meant to be told by a woman, and, obviously by the wyf of Bathe in particular. (Cf D 337-356.) When Chaucer changed

his mind, he forgot to make here the necessary corrections.

Skeat's positive statement that Chaucer himself made the untypically careless error of switching the whole story to a narrator of opposite gender and then forgot to make needed changes in the very beginning, seems strange. It seems doubly strange that neither Skeat nor Tyrwhitt would have thought of the obvious probability that the passage, while assuredly meant for a woman to speak, was out of its rightful place in the manuscript as shown by many misfits other than the obvious ones of the pronouns, and was meant for the Wife of St. Denys to speak as part of her dialogue. Surely it is far more logical, and far simpler, to assume that a damaged manuscript had been hurriedly and carelessly pieced together by the very type of scribe who harrassed Chaucer even during his lifetime than to attribute crass carelessness to Chaucer himself.

Deprived of Chaucer's careful editing by his severe illness or during the years following his death, anything could happen to his manuscripts, just as he feared and prophesied. Obviously this and many less damaging mutilations and careless patchings did occur. But, untypical of the careful scholar as Skeat's positive blame of Chaucer seems to be, quoting from his statement on the assumption that Chaucer was the culprit persists in the architecture and the ornamentation of the House of Straw.

In 1915, George Lyman Kittredge of Harvard followed Skeat in attributing the error to Chaucer, failing to credit (or debit) Skeat. In his first lecture on *The Canterbury Tales* at Johns Hopkins University in Baltimore, Kittredge said:

> The *Shipman's Tale* was originally intended for the Wife of Bath, beyond a doubt . . . .
>
> But Chaucer changed his plan and it is vastly interesting to see his masterpiece gradually taking shape as he goes on with it.[24]

Kittredge ornaments the House of Straw by postulating that the character of the Wife of Bath grew on Chaucer as he wrote the *Shipman's Tale,* so he conceived the idea of devoting a whole act of his human comedy to the discussion of marriage, "and he saw that nobody could be so well-fitted as the Wife of Bath to precipitate such a discussion and control it . . ."

Actually, such a discussion of marriage occurs in Boccaccio's *Decameron,*[25] dealing with the wife's or the husband's dominion in marriage, the chief concern of the tale which the Wife of Bath does in fact relate on the Canterbury Pilgrimage, but which is only a subtle facet, one of several, in the *Shipman's Tale.* Queen Lauretta, presiding over group gatherings of ladies and courtiers in the royal gardens, has each of the group tell a tale. On the seventh day, all the stories have concerned women gaining dominion over men. On the eighth day the queen asks that the narrators relate tales of men tricking women.

Not only does the series concern dominion in marriage, but two tales related on the eighth day, called VIII One and Two, have several points in common with the *Shipman's Tale.* Both are categorized as *fabliaux,* and called "Lover's Gift Regained" stories. In each the wife fools her husband, and her lover is contemptuous enough to risk letting the husband guess that his wife has been unfaithful, in order that the honorable husband may force her to return the money or other gifts which she has received for her "favors." While Neifile, the former queen who has been succeeded by Lauretta, relates the first Eighth Day *Decameron* version of a tale belittling women, it is significant that she has no choice. She has been commanded to tell a story of a woman tricked by a man. Even with this evidence and that of dozens of other similar tales of the "Lover's Gift Regained" type, proving the floating-folktale quality and status of the specific kind of *fabliau* to which the *Shipman's Tale* is consigned, many of which must have been current in Chaucer's time besides the *Shipman's Tale* source, Kittredge actually offers the story's "unmoral tone" as evidence that Chaucer intended it for the Wife of Bath to relate "because it sounds exactly like her."

Seven years after Kittredge delivered his series of Chaucer lectures at Baltimore in 1914-15, Robert Kilburn Root re-echoed the flavor, if not the actual words, of Kittredge's "beyond a doubt." In *The Poetry of Chaucer* Root says:

> Save for its general tone of loose morality, there is no special appropriateness in assigning the tale to the Shipman; and the use of the first person plural in the passage beginning 'he *moot us* clothe and he *moot us* array' shows that it was originally intended for one of the female members of the company, who can have been none other than the wife of Bath. Apparently Chaucer first wrote the tale for her, and then, lighting on another story which would more fully reveal his conception of her character, utilized the rejected tale for the Shipman, forgetting to eliminate the inconsistent passage referred to above.[26]

By 1924, two years later, the House of Straw began wobbling slightly, which is not to be wondered at, considering its growing weight and the guesswork quality of its foundation. John Spiers, in his *Chaucer the Maker,* says:

> The *Shipman's Tale* seems to have been originally intended for a woman.

He goes on to cite the "sely housbonde" couplet with the two "us" pronouns, and then adds:

> . . . whom other than the Wife of Bath? Certainly not . . . the Prioress. A tale originally intended, (it seems) for the Wife of Bath is therefore juxtaposed with a tale by the Prioress.[27]

It will be noted that here the note of positivity is abandoned gracefully. But Dr. Robinson carried over into his 1957 revision of his edition of Chaucer's works the oft-quoted statement in his 1933 edition:

> It is clear from 11. 12-19 that the *Shipman's Tale* was written for a woman, presumably the Wife of Bath.[28]

Yet after this strong assumption that because lines "12-19" were written for a woman to speak the whole Tale was necessarily intended for a woman, the Wife of Bath, to relate, his comment on the entire disputed passage, "lines 4-19" seems much milder:

> Cf. WB. Prol. 11. 337-56. The parallelism of thought, as well as the . . . feminine pronouns, suggests that Chaucer was writing for the Wife.[29]

The citation offered for similarity comparison reads:

Thou seydest also, that if we make us
gay
With clothyng, and with precious array
That it is peril of our chastitee;
And yet, with sorwe! thou must enforce thee,
And seye these wordes in the Apostles name:
'In habit maad with chastitee and shame
Ye wommen shul apparaille yow' quod he,
'And noght in tressed heer and gay peree,
As perles, ne with gold, ne clothes riche.'
After the text, ne after thy rubriche,
I wol not wirche as muchel as a gnat.
Thou seydest this, that I was lyk a
cat
For whoso wold senge a cattes skyn,
Thanne wold the cat wel dwellen in his in;
And if the cattes skyn be slyk and gay
She wol nat dwelle in house half a day.
But forth she wole, or any day be dawed.
To shewe hir skyn, and goon a caterwawed.
This is to seye, if I be gay, sir shrewe
I wol renne out, my borel for to shewe . . .[30]

The only connection, so far as attitude goes, is the fact that women like to wear fine clothing which becomes them. This is true of so many women that it becomes tenuous as a comparison because of its very universality. The only connection so far as language goes is in the use of the word "array" as an end-rhyme word in both the misfit passage in the *Shipman's Tale* and in the passage in which the Wife of Bath is quoting her husband, (not voicing her own philosophy), as accusing women of a cat-like kind of vanity.

She is scolding her husband for his attitude, not slipping out like the Wife of St. Denys to get some other man to "payen for hir cost." As for the use of the word "array," it is an easy word to rhyme, but hardly a characterizing term. Chaucer makes use of it fairly often.

Part III

The Wife Of St. Denys And The Wife Of Bath

A *definite philosophy is expressed* in the misfit lines, 5-19, at the beginning of the *Shipman's Tale.* It is a woman's philosophy, certainly, but that of a sly leaner type of ultra "feminine" woman, one who will get her finery from one man or another, keeping her husband while she fools him.

This is the kind of woman the Wife of St. Denys is, but it is not the Wife of Bath kind of woman. In the dialogue of the Wife of St. Denys, talking to the Monk, trying to get him to supply the cost of clothing (which, she claims unfairly, her husband denies her), this philosophy fits.

The passage is the legalistic type of argument. The Wife of St. Denys placates her husband by argument when he returns from Paris and tells her he is aware that the Monk has "repaid" to her the money borrowed from the husband. She uses a type of humor which should show, by analogy alone, that the argument, in the disputed passage, for "sely housbondes" to recognize the obligation to "clothe and array" their wives, (not to allow them to clothe and array *themselves* as the Wife of Bath demands) is rightfully an additional part of the St. Denys wife's argument to persuade the Monk to lend her a hundred francs. She tells her husband she thought the Monk owed them that much, in return for hospitality, and that having so thought she felt free to spend it for new clothes.[31] Both arguments, the "sely housbonde" passage with the feminine pronouns, and this ingenious argument, have the same logical flavor.

There is an unprincipled kind of humor in both the interpolated first-person passage in the beginning of the *Shipman's Tale* and in the speech of the Wife of St. Denys when she offers, near the close of the Tale, to pay her husband back in something she already owes him—her favors. Note the admission at the start of the tale where the woman speaking says a "compaignable and revelous woman" is a cause of more dispence than she is worth, considering how fleeting is the pleasure she can give, which "passen as doth a shadwe upon a wal." Yet if her husband "noght may" pay for it, she will see to it that another "payen for oure cost." Is this not the type of woman to get a chuckle out of telling her husband she will pay him back for having spent the money he loaned the Monk on finery for herself, but pay him "in no way but abed?"

Conversely, the Wife of Bath is not sly. Her humor is lusty but frank. The women are opposites in nature and in philosophy throughout the Wife's prologue and the tales told by the Shipman and the Wife of Bath. The Shipman tells a stag-yarn type of *fabliau* which makes a woman show herself as dependent, faithless, and sly. Throughout the Wife of Bath's Prologue she shows herself to be self-reliant, militant, frank, and blunt. There are other ways in which each is individual and opposite to the other:

1. The Wife of St. Denys pleads and threatens suicide to get what she wants. She is the "feminine" type of woman.

2. The Wife of Bath boldly demands what she wants. She is the "feministic" woman who scorns masculine opinion, even that of an apostle.

3. The Wife of St. Denys says her motivation for wanting to look her best is to do honor to her husband, an insincere effort to cloak her vanity.

4. The Wife of Bath says truthfully that she dresses up to catch a husband.

5. The Wife of St. Denys is an unprincipled liar, branding as niggardly a husband who has been proved to be the most generous of hosts. His generosity is further proved by his concern at the chance that his friend the Monk might have mistaken his friendly call in Paris for an attempt to collect the hundred francs he has lent him.

6. The Wife of Bath is so lacking in tact and so truthful that she tells the full story of her many husbands, and her quarrels with them, on a pilgrimage during which she hopes to find a sixth husband.

> An housbonde I wol have, I wol not lette,
> Which shal be both my dettour and my thral.[32]

7. The Wife of St. Denys is selfish. She asks for money only for herself and spends it, when she gets it, on clothing for herself.

8. The Wife of Bath is a weaver at the time the *Canterbury Tales* are recounted. She is self-supporting.

She has been generous with her fifth husband, the Clerk of Oxford, making her property over to him. She is self-willed, but generous when she loves.

9. The Wife of St. Denys wants support.

10. The Wife of Bath wants dominion.

The Wife of Bath would hardly have been chosen, even temporarily, by so keen a student of character as Chaucer, to tell a story about the kind of wife appearing in the *Shipman's Tale* and other "Lover's Gift Regained" stories—clinging, sly, easily fooled by a lover too readily trusted and, in her estimation, willing to betray her to avoid repaying money for which he had received value and which he could easily have collected from his parishioners. In her frenzy to justify herself, the Wife of St. Denys was typically unfair. She professed anger at the Monk for telling the Merchant he had "repaid" the loan to her, whereas by so doing he relieved her of her promise to repay it in cash "or any way he listed" and forced the husband to pay for clothing he would have had to buy for his wife in any event. The lover did not regain his "gift" and he risked the Merchant's friendship and the warm hospitality of his home. Tricky and sly as the Wife of St. Denys was, the story remains one of dependent woman and dominant man.

The opposite philosophy of the Wife of Bath was that of the dominion of women over men. The story she did tell was devised to prove that woman's chief desire is "sovereignty" over her husband. So she tells of a knight of Arthur's court who is condemned to die for ravishing a peasant girl, and who is saved temporarily by Guinevere who sends him to find out "what thyng it is that wommen most desyren." He finds that most agree the desirable things are riches and "lust abedde," also prized by the flighty Wife of St. Denys. In the Wife of Bath's story honour is chosen, joliness and frequent marriage, whereas the Wife of St. Denys has specified as "things sixe women naturally desiren," the two specified above, and housbondes free with their money; "buxom, hardy, and wise." However, the point of the Wife of Bath's story is that none of these guesses was right. The proper answer to Queen Guinevere's question was that what women most desire is sovereignty over their husbands. The Knight was unable to solve the riddle and an ugly witch, (the loathly dame of folklore), supplied the answer at a high price: he must marry her. And when, reluctantly, he kept his bargain and she asked him whether he would rather have a fair, young wife who would be untrue to him or an old and ugly wife who would be faithful, he acknowledged her superior wisdom and offered her the mastery over him. Whereupon she changed into a lovely young bride who promised to be true, but she did not yield her dominion.

That is the tale the Wife of Bath told on the Pilgrimage, and it is completely suited to her ruling philosophy. Since she was either a real character known to Chaucer, or his fictive creation, it seems unlikely that he would at any time assign her a story opposite to her philosophy. And the idea that, if he had, he would have been too careless to make changes to justify the shift seems insulting to so careful a craftsman who has faithfully motivated and prepared for his interpolations throughout the *Canterbury Tales*. The disputed passage at the start of the *Shipman's Tale* does not reflect the character of the Wife of Bath, but its opposite. It does reflect the character and philosophy of the Wife of St. Denys.

Part IV

The Shipman

I*f the Shipman's Tale* is not suited to the philosophy of the Wife of Bath, especially the very passage in Lines 5-19, which is the excuse for stating that the whole Tale was originally assigned by Chaucer for her to relate, then to whom is the tale better suited?

Why not, in the name of logic, to the Shipman?

It is a risqué story. It was floating around in many versions at the time Chaucer was writing. It dignifies men and cheapens women. It invites chuckles at the cleverness of rascals who betray friendships and take advantage of weak-moraled women. It is, *per se,* the kind of story which a rascal like the Shipman, as representing the unscrupulous male antagonist in the Battle of the Sexes, would tell to build his own ego-concept and that of his male listeners at roistering drinking parties. It is a typical stag yarn proving how stupid, easily fooled and faithless "the little woman" is and how honest the husband is to see to it that any money paid to her is properly accredited to the account of the lover who has "borrowed" it from him.

Chaucer, an original no matter what his sources, could never fail to enhance and deepen any characterization which he attempted. This is shown by the long-lived popularity of his works over whatever sources he may have used. Enhancing the characters, he has made the wife more sympathetic than other wives in "Lover's Gift Regained" stories. Enhancing the characters of the Canterbury Pilgrims, he has made each one an arch-type of his or her kind. There are several possible avenues of approach available to demonstrate the likelihood that Chaucer assigned the Tale to the Shipman because he had heard it first from a ship's captain, and that he put a shipman on a mainly real or mainly fictional pilgrimage purposely to have him relate a risqué story that was going the rounds at the time, orally at first, later written and printed in the folklore of many countries.

1. What was Chaucer's opportunity to hear the current risqué story from a shipman? As Collector of Customs for wool, hides, tallow, and, later, wine brought to the Port of London, he must have known many ships' captains in the way of transacting business with them. As the son of a wine merchant he would have had some reputation as a connoisseur of wines. As appraiser of the values of the wines on which he collected customs he must have drunk wine with many a ship's captain, during which, as a writer and student of human nature, he must have traded amusing stories with them. As a high-ranking traveler on king's business he would be invited to sit at the Captain's table on the seven or more voyages he made to the European continent. Almost as certainly he would have visited the captain on the bridge or joined him on hilarious and surreptitious visits to the galley at night where wines from cargoes were available.

2. What kind of man, in the round, was the Shipman?

First, we meet him in the General Prologue:

A Shipman was ther, wonynge fer by weste
For aught I woot, he was of Dertemouthe.

He rood upon a rouncy, as he kouthe,
In a gowne of faldyng to the knee.
A daggere hangynge on a laas hadde he
Aboute his nekke, under his arm adoun.
The hoote somer hadde maad his hewe al broun;
And çerteinly he was a good felawe.
Ful many a draughte of wyn had he ydrawe
Fro Burdoux-ward, whil that the chapman sleep.
Of nyce conscience took he no keep.
If that he faught, and hadde the hyer hond,
By water he sente hem hoom to every lond.
But of his craft to rekene wel his tydes,
His stremes, and his daungers hym bisides
His herberwe, and his moone, his lodemenage,
Ther nas noon swich from Hulle to Cartage.
Hardy he was and wys to undertake;
With many a tempest hadde his berd been shake.
He knew alle the havenes, as they were,
Froom Gootlond to the cape of Fynystere.
And every cryke in Britaigne and in Spayne
His barge ycleped was the Maudelayne.[36]

It will be observed that while Chaucer obviously knew a great deal about shipmen in general and, most probably, this Shipman in particular or several of his prototypes, it is much less likely that he met him on a religious pilgrimage than that he met him on a voyage or in the way of customs business. It would have kept Chaucer's Shipman busy, robber and murderer that he was, to make pilgrimages to get forgiveness for his continuous succession of crimes.

Docking a ship accustomed to pirate other ships' cargoes, for the number of days needed to make a land trip by "rouncy" from London to Canterbury and return, would have risked the seizure of the ship to pay for pirated cargoes.[37]

It may be that we see the Shipman next in the Epilogue to the *Man of Law's Tale,* also called the *Shipman's Prologue.* There is so much disagreement as to the assignment of the bit that even if needed for added character revealment it cannot be claimed with certainty for the Shipman.

Two organic clues justify his claim.[38] The passage reads:

> 'Nay, by my fader soule, that schal he nat!'
> Seyde the Shipman; 'heer schal he nat preche;
> He schal no gospel glosen here ne teche.
> We leven alle in the grate God,' quod he;
> 'He wolde sowen som difficulte,
> Or springen cokkel in our clene corn.
> And therefore, Hoost, I warne the biforn
> My joly body schal clynken you so mery a belle,
> That I schal waken al this compaignie.
> But it schal not ben of philosophie,
> Ne physlyas, ne termes queinte of lawe.
> Ther is but litel Latyn in my mawe.'[39]

The courteous Wife of Bath, polite even to the twice-interrupting Pardoner, would not shout against the Parson in this rude tone; not she, who had made many pilgrimages to the Holy Land and other shrines and always married "at chirche dore." The two indications that the speech was meant for the Shipman are: (1) its bold voice of authority fits it for the commander of a pirate ship; (2) "joly body" appears again in line 423 in the *Shipman's Tale.*

Even without the support of the Epilogue, the General Prologue characterization plus his choice of a tale show that the Shipman is not a religion-centered man. As master of a vessel he was empowered to conduct funerals, weddings, and services of other kinds usually performed on land by priests and ministers. He shows a lack of veneration for the clergy just as he shows a lack of respect for merchants' wares entrusted to him. There are many rascals on Chaucer's Canterbury Pilgrimage, as he is first to admit, but none other such arrant thief, killer, and pirate as the Shipman. The Pardoner, for example, admits he is a rascal, but he has a rascally reason for being on the trip; he hopes to sell indulgences and some of his fake relics on the journey and at Canterbury. He defeats his purpose by boasting of his cleverness at deception. The Wife of Bath admits her shortcomings even while hoping to attract a sixth husband.

Conversely, the Shipman seems to be present for the author's convenience, to relate a risqué tale of a currently popular kind which would result, and has resulted, in great popularity for the *Canterbury Tales,* along with its many other recommendations for success. However, Kemp Malone in his *Chapters on Chaucer* and Kittredge, in his lectures at Johns Hopkins where Malone later taught, state opposite opinions on this point. Kittredge said, "The Pilgrims do not exist for the sake of the stories, but vice versa."[40]

Malone wrote:

> . . . the transfer of this tale from the Wife of Bath to the Shipman shows clearly enough that, for Chaucer, the tale was there for its own sake, not for the sake of the teller.[41]

Thus do experts commenting on the *Shipman's Tale* disagree, even the most world-renowned Chaucerians teaching at world-acclaimed universities, each adding his positive statement as fact even when taking opposite stands.

Wherever Chaucer may have met his Shipman, or shipmen from whom he assembled traits to make up his Shipman character, there has long been speculation as to whether the Shipman existed intact in real life. Margaret Galway, in her "Chaucer's Shipman in Real Life" suggests that he was a privateer named John Piers who boarded a boat named the "Magdaleyn" in 1383, killed her crew, threw its members into the ocean, and loaded her cargo on the ship he commanded, the "Ste. Marie." He had to dock his boat at the port of London to wait out a storm and the ship was seized in payment for the sunken "Magdaleyn." One Payn Dorea, supposedly the insurer of the cargo or the ship's owner, was sued for damages.[42]

Piers seems to have been a persuasive rascal. Before the suit was settled, he captained a British admiralty ship, and, with eighteen of his mariners he deserted as soon as convenient. He transferred allegiance from France to England and back as expedience dictated, escaping punishment because of his skill as a navigator and his fearlessness in battle. It will be seen that Piers and Chaucer's Shipman tally on a number of significant points. Each is a pirate and murderer who drowns his defeated adversaries. Each is an outstanding mariner. The name of a boat called the "Maudelayne" or the "Magdalayne" is associated with both. And the time element justifies itself. Robinson's chronology of the writing of Chaucer's works places the General Prologue in which the Shipman is described and characterized, between 1387 and 1392,[43] while the Piers incident is shown by Admiralty records to have taken place in time to serve as material for Chaucer. Its date is the winter of 1383.

Professor Manly theorizes that Chaucer's Shipman was Peter Risshenden, captain of a ship named the "Maudelayne" in 1391. He says this seems to be the same boat which was captained by George Cowntree in 1379. Manly thinks Risshenden is identical with Piers Risselden who, in 1386, commanded the balinger of Dartmouth which helped the privateer "Hawley" capture three "crayers" in the Bay of Ordiorne.[44] If Risshenden used "Piers" as a version of "Peter" and added it to "Risselden" as an alias when in trouble for piracy, barratry and murder, it may be that, in 1383, he used "Piers" as a surname and put "John" before it as an effort to confuse the authorities when legal entanglements grew out of his piracy of the "Magdaleyn." Miss Galway thinks the real John Piers was a Basque and that the allusion to Dartmouth, port of pirates, in Chaucer's *General Prologue* was one of the poet's jokes.

Part V

The Tale Itself

W*hoever the ship's captain* or captains on whom Chaucer based his Shipman may have been in real life, the *fabliau* which Chaucer has him tell is not only fitting for a rough and traveled man like the Shipman of the Pilgrimage to relate, but is obviously the kind of story a ship's captain would tell a genial and interested passenger on his boat. Since Chaucer went to Italy on several of his seven or more trips abroad, it is even probable that he told the story to Boccaccio and that they discussed men's and women's dominion in marriage as a springboard for groups of stories in situation framework.

Boccaccio's First and Second Eighth Day novellas resemble the *Shipman's Tale* in several ways. In *Decameron* VIII-One, the wife of an Italian merchant named Guasperruolo of Milan makes a frank charge of 200 florins for favors which she sells to a German soldier named Gulfardo. He borrows the sum from the woman's rich husband on her promise to admit him to her home as soon as her husband leaves Milan. The soldier is ungallant enough to bring along a witness when he hands over the money, saying to the wife, "Keep this and give it to your husband when he returns."

In spite of this clear clue to his intentions, the woman grants her "favors" to the conniving soldier. And when he tells her husband in her presence that he has "repaid" a loan to her, she cannot deny it, having accepted the money before a witness.[45]

In the second Eighth Day novella, *Decameron* VIII-Two, the faithless friend of the honest husband is a churchman of Verlungo. Boccaccio has the false wife asking the priest for a loan of money while the husband is away on a trip. He tells her he has no cash but gives her a cloak instead and asks her to lend him a mortar. She gives him her "favors" in return for his cloak. When the husband returns the priest tells him he has borrowed a mortar and is sending it back by a messenger, and that he wants the cloak the man's wife has asked him to leave as security for the mortar. Shocked at her miserliness, the husband forces the wife to return the cloak paid her for her favors.[46]

A kind of gentling occurs in Chaucer's relating of the *fabliau* which is not present in other "Lover's Gift Regained" stories—a kind of gallantry.[47]

In his version a wealthy merchant of St. Denys in France, (which locale leads Robinson to argue must indicate a French source for Chaucer's and Boccaccio's versions of the tale),[48] asks a friend, a monk named Daun John, to visit him and his beautiful wife before the merchant leaves for Bruges on business. He sits up all night before the trip casting up his annual accounts, so breakfast is late. The wife strolls in the garden accompanied by an unaccounted-for child, and finds the Monk there, trying to stall off his hunger. He tells her he assumes the breakfast delay means that the husband has kept her awake with his attentions. She tells him he could not be more mistaken; her husband is interested only in money, and at the moment she needs a hundred francs to buy Sunday clothing. If the Monk will not lend it to her she will be "lorn" and must die;

if anyone finds out about the loan she would wish she had never been born.

The Monk borrows the money from the Merchant, telling him he needs it to buy livestock for his monastery. The husband says there is no hurry about repayment; the Monk may take his time and return it "at his ease." He couldn't lend a large amount, since to a chapman "his gold is his plough," but to a hundred francs the Monk is welcome.

The husband has prospered all year and his business in Bruges goes well also. He goes to Paris to see the Monk and learns to his surprise that the loan has been "repaid" to the wife. He is shocked at the thought that perhaps the Monk thinks he came to Paris to collect the money after telling him to take his time repaying it, and is further shocked when he returns to St. Denys and his wife fails to mention the money. He scolds her, and, like all the wives in "Lover's Gift Regained" stories, she reacts in anger, not contrition. She is cured of her love for the Monk. She says she thought he gave her the hundred francs in partial payment for the many times he has visited them in St. Denys; she considered he owed them that much in gratitude. However, the husband shall not lose. Although she has spent the money for new clothes, she will pay it back in affection. The husband seems better off for the whole episode since his straying wife is now back, chastened. A sponging houseguest, most disloyal, will hardly return for further free food and lodging—or will he? The only one worse off, if not, is the Monk, who had everything to lose by finding the money to lend the wife. She will never trust him again. His only motive in telling the husband, if self-centered, would be to avoid repaying the loan, a small sum compared to the hospitality he was receiving. Actually he was freeing the wife from any debt to him by telling the husband the debt was repaid, thus cancelling the whole transaction. And the wife's husband has paid for her new wardrobe.

There is no such careful motivational rounding out in most versions of the "Lover's Gift Regained" stories. The hand of the master shows clearly in the Chaucer version, with double twists at the close of the story. The wife is befooled, and she also befools. The husband is the only noble character in the story whose loyalty is sustained throughout, making it a masculine-slanted story.

In most of the *fabliaux* quoted by Dr. Spargo the wives are crassly commercial, openly selling their favors for money or gifts.[49] There is no mention of repaying the cash value of the goods they collect. Sometimes they never saw the lovers before. Sometimes they meet them in the dark and have no idea of their identities. Some are incredibly stupid, like the wife in *Decameron* VIII-One, yielding to lovers who have proved the intention to betray them. In some versions the lover who borrows money from the husband asks in advance whether he may repay it to the wife in the husband's absence, thereby helping the convincingness of the "repayment" claim, but spoiling the story's surprise ending. In this type and in the Chaucer version the "gift" is not regained by the lover, but by the husband, or is retained by the wife, so the "Lover's Gift Regained" classification must be applied broadly.

Dr. Spargo considers Chaucer's version more primitive than Boccaccio's versions.[50] While it seems likely that Chaucer heard it independently from a ship's captain but may well have told it to Boccaccio or discussed it with him while on a visit to Italy, the fact that Chaucer streamlined instead of cluttering his character-cast, while expanding character-motivations, seems to show his more advanced craftsmanship. His simpler arrangements for the "repaying" of the loan and the lack of witnesses or pledges, also seem more clear-cut and advanced. Many stories of the category, besides the *Decameron* VIII-Two, have elaborate pledge devices and bartered articles such as cloth, gold bars, horses-and-wagons, and shoes as "gifts." The cash payment in Chaucer's story shows the evolution from barter to money. The motives of the wives in the Boccaccio novelles and many other versions seem cruder and more primitive than those of the Wife of St. Denys. They are so miserly that they still have the money or gift intact when the lover demands repayment or credit for repayment. The St. Denys wife's lack of miserliness was her gain; she has spent the hundred francs on woman's feminine weakness, finery. She shows a tricky and humorous but endearing honorableness in offering promptly to "repay" her husband for the money she spent, though she owes him her "favors" and he owes her a Spring wardrobe without the formality of an agreement. This is a double twist that none of Spargo's other quoted *fabliaux* possess.

The widespread status of the basic story told by the *Shipman* shows that claiming the story to be "beyond a doubt" or "doubtless" intended by Chaucer for the Wife of Bath to relate because "it sounds exactly like her" or because it "suits her character" seems naive in view of the many people who have told the multiplicity of versions who were *not* the wife of Bath. Dr. Spargo found fifty versions in Scandinavia alone, in most of which the gift was a pair of pretty shoes. The four exceptions in that region were two instances where the "lover" gave the wife a grouse, one instance of a gold watch as a gift, and one story in which the gift was a cow.[51]

The "Lover's Gift Regained" stories spread in the time of Chaucer and Boccaccio and later when printing became customary, throughout Western civilization. The quick scattering of the basic tale throughout the European and Scandinavian countries and the British Isles shows the agency of widely traveled people as tellers of the story. The most traveled were ship's captains, pilgrims, and merchants. Undoubtedly ship's captains ranged widest in point of travel scope.

No doubt they told Geoffrey Chaucer many versions of the *fabliau* during his successive voyages and during their business visits to his customs office.

In all its versions quoted by Spargo, the story is a male-slanted story, claiming sovereignty for husbands.

Part VI

Other Protesting Voices

While *it has been overlooked* up to now that there is a possibility and even a strong likelihood that the otherwise puzzling feminine pronouns and the otherwise marring misfits of viewpoint and syntax show the disputed lines 5-19 of the *Shipman's Tale* to be a misplaced part of the dialogue of the Wife of St. Denys, there has been evidence of dissatisfaction with the bold assumption that the whole Tale was meant to be related by the Wife of Bath.

Robert L. Chapman, of the State University of New York and Teacher's College, (Oswego, N.Y.), states outright: "The *Shipman's Tale* Was Meant for the Shipman."[52]

He quotes Kittredge's "rule of judgment" in which the late Harvard professor says:

> We perceive in the great poet not a vast, irregular, untaught genius—an amiable but terrible infant, impatient of regulation, acknowledging no laws of structure, guided by no canons of criticism. Quite the contrary! Chaucer was a conscientious student of literary form . . .

> From these considerations there emerges a rule of judgment that is of some value for our guidance in interpreting Chaucer's final masterpiece, *The Canterbury Tales.* It may be stated in the simplest language: *Chaucer always knew what he was about.*[53]

Chapman makes use of Professor Kittredge's "rule of judgment" to refute Kittredge's own argument that the *Shipman's Tale* was "beyond a doubt" assigned originally to the Wife of Bath. Stating that the simplest hypothesis may not always be the best, and assuming that reassignment accompanied by neglect on Chaucer's part *is* the simplest hypothesis, Chapman offers a substitute explanation. However, in groping for a more elaborate explanation, he overlooks the simplest solution of all and proposes one which would undoubtedly win first prize for elaborateness were it not based on the solution already hinted at by von Düring as a bare possibility.[54]

Chapman writes:

> The evidence supporting the standard opinion is, first, the feminine pronouns of lines 12-19.[55] A woman obviously speaks those lines, therefore a woman speaks the tale. Second, since all the other women of the pilgrimage are nuns, and not likely to tell such a rude story, the speaker must be the Wife of Bath.
>
> To begin with the pronouns. They are undeniably feminine, and they undeniably help represent a wifely point of view on the economy of wedlock. But they follow, significantly, a husbandly point of view of the same. These lines, 5-10, are a pendant to the speaker's compact description of the Wife of St. Denys, and with lines 12-19 they form a kind of diptych, on one side the burgher, on the other the burgher's wife. We know, from the General Prologue that the Shipman is a good fellow, that is, an excellent companion on the way. It is likely that he can tell an entertaining story with some flair, even with touches of mimicry. Such a raconteur would speak the burgher's lines in a rueful basso, and the wife in a piping falsetto, and

> thus fitly set the characters and the theme of his story. This is precisely what the Shipman does, and such a reading transforms one of Chaucer's 'inconsistencies' into a slight but pleasing dramatic stroke.

Here, in footnotes, Chapman cites von Düring as quoted by Miss Hammond, and also mentions that Raymond Preston, in his *Chaucer,* casually states the theory proposed in this note: " . . . We have the Shipman comically imitating a woman's voice."[56] Chapman goes on to say:

> Thus for the pronouns. The tale was not intended to be told by a woman, but by a miming male. In what respect is it peculiarly appropriate to the Shipman? We know that by his trade he deals directly with merchants, more directly than any other member of the pilgrimage except the Merchant himself. We know from the General Prologue that his relations with the worshipful chapmen are likely to have been soured by his habit of stealing their wine. *The Shipmen's Tale* is told against a merchant and the Shipman had a better reason than any of the others for making game of that brotherhood.
>
> Certainly he had a better reason than the Wife of Bath had, by what we know of her. Moreover, unless Chaucer altered his idea of Alison entirely during the development of the Canterbury Tales, the *Shipman's Tale* is quite specifically inappropriate to her. The doctrine of women embodied in the tale is unrelievedly masculine, the normal anti-feminist doctrine of the fabliau. In the wife's Prologue and Tale Chaucer's most conspicuous triumph is the transformation of anti-feminist materials into a case for the single standard, for the cosmic credit of womanhood; one is tempted to say for the 'power' and the 'rights' of women. The Wife of Bath would never, without working her peculiar chemistry, have retailed such an example of male bias as the *Shipman's Tale.* It was meant to be told by the shipman.

William W. Lawrence answers Chapman in a paper

called "the Wife of Bath and the Shipman" in *Modern Language Notes* of February 1957.[57] He cites Manly's explanation that "a good felawe," so far from meaning "an excellent companion by the way" actually indicates a rascal. He mentions other uses of the term "a good felawe" in the *Canterbury Tales* to show that Chaucer habitually uses the term ironically. He adds:

> Again, if Chaucer had intended to represent by a change of voice a male and a female speaker, we should expect some definite evidence of this in the text. What has not been clear to most modern critics with their sharp eyes is not likely to have been clear to Chaucer's contemporaries.[58]

And, since Chaucer was a competent and high-ranking customs official and therefore in charge of books in a post calling for completeness and accuracy of records, we should also expect some definite mention to that effect if he had intended the *Shipman's Tale* to be shifted from one narrator (female) to another narrator (male). We should also expect him to have chosen, in that instance, a tale which would fit either. Chaucer has proven himself over and over to be a careful editor. His careful transitions and his anxious and impatient note to his scrivener show this, even if his care were not evident throughout the *Canterbury Tales*.

The misplacement of the disputed lines at the start of the *Shipman's Tale* might well be an indication of his careful editing. If Chaucer felt that the Wife of St. Denys needed an extra bit of argument to persuade her husband's friend, the Monk, to lend her a hundred francs, he might logically have penned an insert to go into her dialogue and attached it to the manuscript of the story. Being a careful man, he would have notated the passage for the lines inside the dialogue where he wanted it inserted. But careless handling could well have resulted in this insert being torn in two in transit, or by scribes or copyists, by manuscript pirates, or by people shuffling through Chaucer's papers during his illness or after his death. The poet's death interrupted the completion of his *Canterbury Tales.*

Of his method of working when in health, while engaged in making his version of *Troilus and Criseyde,* Robert Kilburn Root says, as quoted by Charles A. Owen, Jr., of the University of Connecticut:

> The poet's own draft of his poem, confused, it would seem, on many a page by erasures and interlineations, was turned over to a professional scribe who made a fair copy. This copy contained not only the errors which are inevitable in the work of transcription, but others which arose from Adam's failure to understand here and there his employer's final intention, obscured as it was by a tangle of rewritings and blotted lines. When the poet had 'proof-read' this copy, correcting all of Adam's errors which caught his attention, it became what we may call his own 'official' text from which new copies were made for presentation to friends and patrons.
>
> In this official text the poet also made from time to time other alterations dictated by his exacting poetic instinct—the addition of new passages, the rearrangement of other passages, the new turning of a phrase, the substitution of what seemed to him a happier word, the metrical revision of a halting line.[59]

This patience and conscientiousness with regard to the rightness of all his work seems to be borne out by Chaucer's care in assigning his stories in the *Canterbury Tales* to Pilgrims suited to relate them. He assigns to the Prioress a tale of a little choir boy martyred while singing a prayer. He assigns to the Knight a tale of knightly rivalry and adventure. He has the crude Miller relate a tale ridiculing a carpenter and has the Reeve, himself a carpenter, tell a story making rude sport of a miller. He assigns to himself a boring story so he can create a conflict and show himself modestly as being rudely interrupted. He assigns to the Shipman a story of a man's integrity and a woman's deceitfulness. It is the kind of a story "a good felawe" such as Chaucer showed the rascally Shipman to be would naturally tell, a *fabliau* in which a rascally monk deceived his best friend, a merchant. The disrespect for the clergy shown by the selection of a monk in a deceiver's role gives support to the selection of the story for the sinful Shipman to relate. It would also seem to support the Shipman's claim to the Man of Law's Epilogue, a speech made by a dominant man, used to giving orders, a man scornful of the clergy. He assigned to the Wife of Bath a tale justifying the kind of woman's dominion which she says she held over the best of her many husbands.

The recent articles quoted show that increasing interest is being taken of late in the *Shipman's Tale* puzzle.

Speculating on the direct evidence of the tales and the characterizations of the Pilgrims, as set forth in the Prologues and the Tales, would seem to be more profitable and justifiable than perpetuating admitted guesses from authority to authority.

Speaking of the impossibility of using spelling and punctuation by early copyists in their efforts to patch together notes and mutilated manuscripts, due to the absence of "pointing" in Chaucer's day and to the lack of authenticated examples of Chaucer's own handwriting, Professor Root says definitely:

> No scrap of his own handwriting has survived, nor any MS of any of his writings which we can believe that he ever saw with his own eyes.[60]

Perhaps, one day, the hypothetical ancestor of the fragmentary, incomplete manuscripts of the *Canterbury Tales* will turn up in some musty medieval papers among dusty and neglected accumulations in the attic or cellar of a palace, town house or castle, or may even be found buried in the ground when war or excavation for new buildings uncovers old archives.

Until then, does it not seem simpler and fairer to assume that the manywise misfit passage in the *Shipman's*

Tale is an intended insert, out of place and transposed within itself in existing manuscripts, than to make the repeated accusation that Chaucer would assign it unsuitably in the first place, re-assign it without due notation to that effect, and then "forget" to make alterations of such crucial matters as pronoun number and gender, viewpoint inconsistencies, interrupted introductions of main characters and widely split syntax, all errors occurring together in one easily noticed fifteen-line passage very early in the story?

As Professor Kittredge said, (refuting thereby his own accusation that Chaucer made this multiple error), Chaucer does know what he is about.

His superb technique in constructing his tale tellings, from the standpoint of skilled presentation, is self-evident. His care is attested to in literally hundreds of instances in *The Canterbury Tales.* This should show that he would neither have made an uncharacteristic assignment of the *Shipman's Tale* to the Wife of Bath, nor have forgotten to do the necessary editing if he had re-assigned it to any drastically different character on second thought.

The accusation that he did is that of critics quoting each other; no such accusal is shown by the best evidence, the Tale itself. The indication there is that Chaucer edited carefully but that the "master" manuscript was somehow poorly and even criminally botched in the reassembling of bits after serious mutilation, or that a torn-out marginal note intended for the Wife of St. Denys as dialogue in speaking to the Monk was thenceforth copied erroneously into the beginning of the story.

Further, the strong indication is that this happened during Chaucer's last illness or after his death, so that the poor job of patching the insert and wrongly inserting it was never seen by him.

One need only look at the improvement in unity of style, in syntax, in consistency of gender, in sustained viewpoint and in sustained flavor, as well as at the added strength of the arguments of the Wife of St. Denys, once the rearranged section is restored to her dialogue, to see the clear indication as to where the presently misfit passage belongs; that is, in the Wife's speech to the Monk in the garden of the Merchant's home in St. Denys.

Notes

[1]Fred Norris Robinson (ed.), *The Works of Geoffrey Chaucer,* rev. ed., Boston, Houghton Mifflin Co., 1957.

[2]*Ibid.,* p. 156, line 19.

[3]*Ibid.,* pp. 157-158.

[4]Eleanor Prescott Hammond and Peter Smith, *Chaucer, a Bibliographical Manual,* New York, The Macmillan Co., 1933, p. 473. The other improvements credited to Chaucer by Nott are: rejecting alliteration; introducing the 7-line heroic stanza; and substituting the 10-syllabled line for the Alexandrine.

[5]Robinson, *op. cit., Troilus and Criseyde,* p. 479, lines 1793-1800.

[6]Robinson, *op. cit.,* p. 534.

[7]The split-rhyme line, "Or lene us gold and that is perilous" has been omitted here; as the final line of the transferred misfit passage, it is the only sacrifice.

[8]Robinson, *op. cit.,* p. 157.

[9]John Webster Spargo, "Chaucer's *Shipman's Tale: The Lover's Gift Regained," Folklore Fellows Communications* 91, Helsinki, Suomalainen Teideskatemin Societes (Scientarium) Fennice, 32:7 ff.

[10]Giovanni Boccaccio, *The Decameron,* London, Henry F. Bumpus, 1906, vol. 2, pp. 176-179 has a witness as a fourth character in Novelle VIII-I.

[11]*Ibid.,* Novelle VIII-2, has a messenger as the fourth character, pp. 180-185.

[12]Robinson, *op. cit.,* pp. xxiv-xxv.

[13]Thomas R. Lounsbury, *Studies in Chaucer,* New York, Harper & Bros., 1892, I:94-96.

[14]John Matthews Manly and Edith Rickert, *The Text of the Canterbury Tales,* Chicago, University of Chicago Press, 1940, vol. 2, pp. 46-47.

[15]Manly and Rickert, *op. cit.,* vol. 4, p. 107.

[16]*Ibid.,* p. 68

[17]Manly and Rickert, *op. cit.,* vol. 4, p. 49.

[18]In Robinson's 1957 edition the "Er he to Brugges" line is on p. 156, line 61.

[19]*Ibid.*, line 72.

[20]Manly and Rickert, *op. cit.*, p. 503.

[21]Eleanor Prescott Hammond and Peter Smith, *Chaucer, a Bibliographical Manual*, New York, The Macmillan Co., 1933, pp. 284-285.

[22]Walter W. Skeat, *The Complete Works of Geoffrey Chaucer*, Oxford, Oxford University Press, 1894, pp. 420-421.

[23]Fred Norris Robinson (ed.), *The Works of Geoffrey Chaucer*, rev. ed., Boston, Houghton Mifflin Co., 1957. Robinson numbers these lines 12-19, 14 and 17, p. 156.

[24]George Lyman Kittredge, *Chaucer and His Poetry*, Cambridge, Harvard University Press, 1936, p. 150.

[25]Giovanni Boccaccio, *The Decameron*, London, Henry F. Bumpus, 1906, vol. 2, pp. 179-180.

[26]Robert Kilburn Root, *The Poetry of Chaucer*, Boston, Houghton Mifflin Co., 1922, p. 188.

[27]John Spiers, *Chaucer the Maker*, London, Faber and Faber, 1924, p. 178.

[28]Robinson, *op. cit.*, p. 732. Actually, the "sely housbonde" passage starts with line eleven.

[29]*Ibid*, p. 733. The entire passage begins with line 5.

[30]Robinson, *op. cit.*, p. 79, lines 337-356.

[31]Fred Norris Robinson (ed.), *The Works of Geoffrey Chaucer; Shipman's Tale*, rev. ed., Boston, Houghton Mifflin Co., 1957, p. 160, lines 406-424.

[32]Ibid., *The Wife of Bath's Prologue*, pp. 77,11. 154-155.

[36]Fred Norris Robinson (ed.,), *The Works of Geoffrey Chaucer*, "General Prologue," p. 21, lines 388-410.

[37]Margaret Galway, in "Chaucer's Shipman in Real Life," *Modern Language Review*, 34:497-514, October 1939, gives such an instance of confiscation.

[38]Robinson, *op. cit.*, notes, p. 696. Robinson says the ML epilogue is assigned in many MSS to the Squire but is unsuited to him; that Brusendorff favors the Yeoman, and "In a single copy, (Ms. Arch. Seld) only is the *Shipman's Tale* preceded by the ML epilogue. Hammond, *op. cit.*, makes the same statement. Selden B. 14 is the ms. indicated. J. S. P. Tatlock, "Order of the Canterbury Tales," PMLA, 50:100-141, p. 117ff., March 1935, argues that the *Shipman's Prologue* was written by Chaucer to precede the *Shipman's Tale.*

[39]Robinson, *op. cit.*, p. 75, lines 1178-1190.

[40]George Lyman Kittredge, *Chaucer and His Poetry*, Cambridge, Harvard University Press, 1936, p. 150.

[41]Kemp Malone, *Chapters on Chaucer,* Baltimore, Johns Hopkins Press, 1951, p. 217.

[42]Galway, *op. cit.,* p. 497 ff.

[43]Robinson, *op. cit.* The chronology of Chaucer's works is in his introduction on p. xxix.

[44]John Matthews Manly, *Some New Light on Chaucer,* New York, Henry Holt & Co., 1926, p. 179.

[45]Giovanni Boccaccio, *The Decameron,* London, Henry F. Bumpus, 1906, vol. 2, pp. 176-179.

[46]*Ibid.,* vol. 2, pp. 180-185.

[47]Fred Norris Robinson (ed.), *The Works of Geoffrey Chaucer,* rev. ed., Boston, Houghton Mifflin Co., 1957. The *Shipman's Tale* is on pp. 156-160.

[48]*Ibid.,* notes, The *Shipman's Tale,* p. 732.

[49]John Webster Spargo, *"Chaucer's Shipman's Tale: The Lover's Gift Regained," Folklore Fellows Communications* 91, Helsinki, Suomalainen Teiderkatemn Societes (Scientarium) Fennice, 32:7 ff.

[50]*Ibid.,* pp. 47 ff.

[51]*Ibid.,* p. 52.

[52]Robert L. Chapman, "The *Shipman's Tale* Was Meant for the Shipman," *Modern Language Notes,* 81:4-5, January 1956.

[53]George Lyman Kittredge, *Chaucer and His Poetry,* Cambridge, Harvard University Press, 1936, p. 150.

[54]Eleanor Prescott Hammond and Peter Smith, *Chaucer, a Bibliographical Manual,* New York, The Macmillan Co., 1933, pp. 284-285.

[55]Here Chapman has omitted line eleven, an omission perpetuated by commentators from the notes in the Robinson texts, *op. cit.* The passage is in Lines Eleven-Nineteen, text of the *Shipman's Tale,* both Robinson editions; p. 156, revised edition.

[56]Raymond Preston, *Chaucer,* London, Sheed & Ward, 1952, p. 205, cited by Chapman, *op. cit.*

[57]William W. Lawrence, "The Wife of Bath and the Shipman," *Modern Language Notes,* 71:4-5, February 1957.

[58]John Matthews Manly, *Canterbury Tales by Geoffrey Chaucer,* New York, 1928, p. 534. Manly's definition reads: "A disreputable fellow; a rascal." Quoted by Lawrence, *ibid.*

[59]Robert Kilburn Root, *The Book of Troilus and Cresyde by Geoffrey Chaucer,* Princeton, Princeton University Press, 1945, p. xxvii, as quoted in Charles A. Owen, Jr., "Chaucer's Method of Composition," *Modern Language Notes,* 72:164, March 1957.

[60]Robert Kilburn Root, *The Book of Troilus and Cresyde by Geoffrey Chaucer,* Princeton, Princeton University Press, 1945, p. xxxiv.

Natalie Grimes Lawrence

Quem quaeritis

L*iturgical drama arose out* of Medieval man's concern with the cross and the crèche of Jesus Christ: first, the Resurrection after the crucifixion and death, and developing somewhat later in the drama, the birth in the manger. From the fourth century the Mass had been the central and most sublime rite in the liturgy, itself, commemorating in the fraction and commixture the death and resurrection of the Lord Jesus.

Small wonder that on Easter Sunday there should in time have been added an expansion of the Mass in the form of a short play, performed at the altar just prior to the Introit, and called *De Resurrectione Domini* in the earliest extant version, the St. Gall MS 484, which appears in Adams[1] under the title it is best known by, *The Quem-Quaeritis Trope.* For the dialogue, in song, begins with the demand of the angels guarding the tomb: *Quem quaeritis in sepulchro* [ǫ] *Christicolae?"* The answer by the three Marys, to this question of whom they are seeking, is "Jesus of Nazareth;" and something of their shocked mourning declares itself in the added words, "which is crucified." But the angels meet this grief by singing trumphantly that He is risen, just as had been foretold, and give command that the glad tidings be spread abroad that Christ is risen from the sepulchre. One can easily picture the impact of the acted version of the familiar story upon the worshippers, the very excision of which heightened its moving quality. Moreover though presented in Latin as was the liturgy, yet the impersonation of the three Marys and of the Angels by the monks, the representation of the sepulchre and the movement towards it, the beauty of the sung dialogue, the very emotion of those taking the parts must have pierced the hearts of those who looked and listened. For most of them knew of Latin only a word or two dinned into them by the patient clergy to help in following the service—one fears, but stumblingly with reliance rather upon the intoning of the priest, the antiphons of the choir, and the pervasive incense to feed in them the awe which the call to worship had stirred.

From the time of the Carolingian Renaissance in the ninth century there were many tropes or elaborations of the liturgy, but of them all the *Quem quaeritis* described above seems to have been the first to develop into drama, growing in its later forms into a grasp of character combined with dramatic intensity which perhaps gives allowance for saying that this trope was the beginning of modern drama.

By the eleventh and twelfth centuries tropes from St. Gall, Limoges, St. Magloire, and Nevers; from Mantua, Bobbio, and Padua celebrate the birth of Christ in the *Pastores.* The Gospel of Luke (ii, 7-20) serves as direct source of these plays, though Matthew (ii, 1-11) star-points the story as it does that of the Magi. The dialogue had to be devised, and the Easter introit trope, *Quem quaeritis,* seems to have been the model.[2] The eleventh century text from Limoges (Paris, Bibl. Nat., MSlat. 877) shows the dependency, beginning: "*Quem quaeritis in praesepe, pastores, dicite?*" The praesepe, the crèche or manger, in these plays becomes the center about which they are built just as the sepulchre was for the Easter play. From these centers the Easter and Christmas plays were inevitably committed to treat of birth, death and transcendent life: material which humanity has always felt the need to deal with and of which drama has not tired. James Matthew Manly puts it that medieval drama is "an art as spacious and hospitable as the medieval church."[3] Well known today is the spread of that art over most of Romanized Europe and in England and Ireland. Manly and Sir E. K. Chambers by the first part of this century had made easily accessible to the English reader the beautiful development of the Easter drama in the *Regularis Concordia Monarchorum,* the date of which Chambers takes as somewhere between 965 and the death of Edgar in 975. This "liberal scenario," as Chambers calls it, was probably devised by Ethelwold, who became Bishop of Winchester in 963. Familiar as it is, evidences of its artistry should be noted in the prose directions for the performance. First, "one vested in an alb," a white linen vestment, goes toward the sepulchre and sits quietly there with a palm in his hand. The three approach him "like folk lost and seeking something." Then the white robed angel begins to sing the *Quem quaeritis* "in a dulcet voice of medium pitch." Further action and song minutely detailed follow to the point where the *Te Deum laudamus* is hymned, and "This begun, all the bells chime sweetly together."[4] So gracious a spirit has molded this scenario that its beneficence remains undiminished. However except for the Winchester and Dublin tropes such plays as there probably were in the English church have perished, either at the hands of Henry the Eighth's wreckers or through other exigencies of time.

Yet fuller development of the dramatic potentials of the Introit trope was to take place, however, as the manuscripts from Western Europe, particularly from France, testify. As part of the Mass, this trope was overshadowed by the liturgy itself. Gradually separation between them began. The place of the *Quem quaeritis* was moved to the procession, which on days of liturgical importance followed terce (9:00 A.M.) and preceded Mass. To give a visual conception of this ceremony, Young summarizes the rubric of the thirteenth century text from Monza, the ancient capital of Lombardy:

> The procession enters the basilica and advances towards the choir during the triple repetition of the antiphon *Et valde mane.* As the singers and clergy enter the choir, a crown of lights of candles and cotton is set ablaze over a gilded cross. The dramatic dialogue now takes place before the altar. Near the altar is a faldstool covered with a drapery to represent the sepulchre. Standing beside this two clerics vested in copes represent the angels and two other clerics similarly vested represent the Marys. With the familiar dialogue the procession is concluded . . . the Mass begins.[5]

From the procession the *Quem quaeritis trope* moved again—to the Canonical hours—finding appropriate place between Matins (ending at dawn) and Lauds, as the visit to the sepulchre itself figures forth an event occuring traditionally at dawn of Easter day. With the transfer to the processional where the trope was nearer the liturgical offices of the *Depositio* and *Elevatio,* the *Quem quaeritis in sepulchro* underwent the development into the more liberally contrived play entitled in some manuscripts and early printed books, *Visitatio Sepulchri.* Attesting to the pleasure of the worshippers in the truly dramatic presentation of this play is the large number of manuscripts and early printings still preserved. As early as the tenth century the impersonation rather than mere representation had begun: a movement destined to gain strength up to the peak of liturgical drama in the mid-thirteenth century. From the texts that remain there seem to be three stages of growth indicated in the Easter play, all pointing toward a surer grasp and illumination of character: (1) Amplification of the dialogue between the Marys and the Angels (2) Addition of the apostles Peter and John as characters in the drama (3) The giving of a role to the risen Christ; and the use of Roman soldiers, somewhat individualized, to guard the tomb.[6]

Something of the development in length, in dramatic intensity and characterization during the twelfth and thirteenth centuries—and beyond—may perhaps become clearer through a close view of four notable Easter plays. Young provides a copy in Latin or Latin and the vernacular, as the case may be, for these plays.[7] The following somewhat abbreviated versions have been "englyshed" by the writer of this essay. The plays to be considered are the play from the monastery for women at Origny-Sainte Benoit, near St. Quentin; the *Ordo Paschalis* from Klosterneuberg, near Vienna; the *Carmina Burana* play from the monastery at Benediktbeuern, in Bavaria; and the Easter play from Tours.

The Origny-Sainte Benoit manuscript (St. Quentin, Bibl. de la Ville, M886 *olim* 75) shows a marked transitional trend in that both dialogue and rubrics appear partly in Latin, partly in French. With the use of the vernacular there comes into the play a homely plaintiveness which intensifies the humanness of the characters. For instance, when the three Marys mourn their beloved dead they say that they have lost their comfort, who was so fair and full of kind love. When they go to purchase the ointment for the preservation of Christ's body they are urgent that the merchant, now a gentle merchant, sell them the best that he has; then they groan in remembrance that alas! they shall see their Christ never again. The merchant eagerly tries to help them in honoring the 'tres grant Seigneur.'

At the tomb a variant of the *Quem quaeritis* follows in Latin but is succeeded by a very moving scene between the two Angels and Mary Magdalen whom they address in French as "sweet lady, who so weeps." After further converse with her the pitying Angels again address her as "Douce dame" and tell her that immediately the King Jesus will see her and will assuage her sorrow. Christ himself appears to her and to the other Marys. A dialogue ensues in Latin. Then Christ turning to Mary Magdalen asks: "Woman, why do you weep? Whom do you seek?" Not recognizing him, she makes her plea to be told where those who have taken her Lord away have placed him. Christ calls her name: "Maria." Throwing herself at his feet, she cries out: "Raboni!"

The command is given to all the Marys to go spread the word. They inform the chorus that Christ is risen. The apostles John and Peter rush to the sepulchre and bring forth the grave cloths. At this point the text breaks off leaving but a fragmentary ending, perhaps followed by such an antiphon as *Surrexit Dominus de Sepulchro,* which Young suggests, with that being followed, as Coussemaker assumed, by the *Te Deum.* Certainly there is an intimacy of feeling expressed in the vernacular portions of this play not met with in the earlier tropes. The manuscript is found in the record of customs of the monastery for the thirteenth and fourteenth centuries.

The *Ordo Paschalis* from Klosterneuberg (Stiftsbibl. ms 574) has come down to us written in two hands of the early thirteenth century. The manuscript is in Latin except for one line and the Germanized refrain of the soldier's song. Perhaps the strongest aspect of its dramatic development is the presentation of the Harrowing of Hell. Although the manuscript is defective it includes with some variations the usual parts of the Easter play. It opens with Pontius Pilate seating himself in the place "preordained;" he is joined by his officers singing. Pilate sends the soldiers to stand guard over Christ's sepulchre. They march about it singing. As their song sinks into silence an Angel comes upon them, wheels from left to right with a sword, and sings that the Victor is arisen from the dead. The Angel then strikes one of the soldiers with the sword; he and all the others fall prone upon the earth. The play proceeds along usual lines, but after Mary Magdalen's exit, Christ is led by two Angels preceding him to the infernal gates. There he sings the well known antiphon *Tollite portas:* "Open up the gates . . . and let the King of Glory in."

Whereupon the Devil thrice sounds the expected question "Who is this King of Glory?" The answer comes back: "The Lord strong and powerful, the Lord powerful in battle."

With a violence of action not customary in the acted role of Christ, He Who is the Lord of Glory, breaks down the gates. The imprisoned spirits rush to welcome Him, and sing *Advenisti desiderablis.* The rest of the manuscript seems to return upon itself with a re-entry of Mary Magdalen and the other Marys plus the Apostles Peter and John all rejoicing by word or song that Christ is risen. Comes the one excursion into the vernacular; now that the whole people have been assured concerning the Lord, the leader of the choir begins their Easter hymn: "Christ, der ist erstanden." Although the manuscript is somewhat disordered, the scenes between Pilate and his soldiers, the Angel with the sword overcoming the braggart soldiers, the terse presentation of the Harrowing of Hell and the sharply dramatic statement in the vernacular of the hymn move toward dramatic intensification close to the worshippers. And the role of Christ sets forth a power hardly met within previous characterization.

In the famous *Carmina Burana* manuscript, found in 1803 at the monastery of Benediktbeuern, is an Easter play wholly in Latin identical in large part with the Klosterneuberg play; yet the Benediktbeuern play is more ample dramatically and more skillful. The play opens with the singing of Easter Matins, and a kind of procession moves toward the place where the sepulchre is. Not only Pilate but his wife as well as the pontiffs and attendants take their places. The soldiers are somewhat individualized as first, second, third, fourth, and fifth.[8] When they have been assigned to their duty of guarding the tomb, they sing four lines in unison, then circle the tomb where each sings individually his disbelief in the predicted rising of Jesus and asserts his determination to keep anyone from carrying off the body. Upon them come two Angels, one bearing a flaming sword and wearing a red garment; the other, clothed in white, carrying the cross in his hand. The Angel with the sword strikes one of the soldiers on the helmet. There is a great sound of thunder, and the soldiers fall as dead. The Angels stand before the tomb and announce, singing, "*Alleluia, Resurrexit victor ab inferis . . .*"

There follows the scene between the Marys and the Apothecary, but this time the apothecary has his wife with him; it is she who looks after the price of the ointment jibing a little at his impracticality. He, however, persists in his gentleness and after the Marys buy the ointment courteously shows them the way to the sepulchre.

The Marys walk about the tomb singing together their deprivation and misery without consolation; they liken themselves to wandering sheep without a shepherd, Him, the people of Palestine have given a cruel death. One Mary sings, "O Deus," then another, then the third. All together they burst into the antiphon, *Quis revolvet nobis lapidum*... This song seems to revive the soldiers, for they go running off to Pilate and the pontiffs to tell them that Christ is risen. They bribe the soldiers not to pass the word along, quite in reverse of the usual Angelic command to spread the good tidings, and here the play ends. A note in the margin of the manuscript by the *Alleluia, Resurrexit victor ab inferis* . . . states that at this point Christ rises from the tomb and takes a speaking part. But the rest is silence and no one knows whether or not this marginal note was relative to a part of the play actually ever performed.

The Easter play from the Diocese of Tours (Tours, Bibl. de la Ville, ms 927) is wholly in Latin. Although the text is somewhat fragmentary, yet in its present state the manuscript shows marked realization of dramatic possibilities and creates such empathic response in the reader that easily can he see how the play must have stirred the beholder. As the play opens, Pilate is convening his soldiers to instruct them to watch the tomb with care. He warns them that the disciples are telling the people that Christ will arise from the dead. The soldiers proud in their charge, go toward the sepulchre singing in unison their threats against any who come to the tomb and emphasizing that at any attempt to transfer the body the soldiers will attack with spears and will strike with swords those who seek to do so. Immediately an Angel (only one) hurls lightning at the soldiers who fall upon the earth as dead.

The three Marys appear, each specifically named in this manuscript: Mary Magdalen, Mary Jacobi, and Mary Salome. Mary Magdalen begins to sing, "Omnipotent Father, most High." Each of the others sings a verse. The last line of each of the three verses underlines their sorrow, *"Heu! Quantus est noster dolor."* While Mary Magdalen has prayed only to know who has done this grievous thing, Mary Jacobi and Mary Salome are concerned to buy ointment to fill the ampules they bear in their hands, for they would protect Christ's body from the "worms." At once appears the merchant who with an eye to business invites them to come buy the ointment which they desire and which he wishes to sell, for he has ointment of great powers against decay. At the word the Marys can only raise their lament again, *"Heu! Quantus est noster dolor!"* Then one of the Marys, specified only as *Marie* (scribal lapse into French form or whatever) asks the Merchant, calling him "Young Merchant," if he will sell them this precious ointment. Here Karl Young[9] sees not the first merchant but his apprentice, making for the first time two merchants in this now traditional scene. Whether or not there be two, the dialogue continues between the Marys and one designated only as the Merchant; they must have an ointment that is aromatic, they assure him. A more or less constant accompaniment to this dialogue is the lament (*Heu! quantus est noster dolor!*)[10] making a very striking effect of grief-stricken song enveloping the purchase to be used in such sad office, providing something of orientation of emotion comparable to that of the Greek chorus. Finally the purchase accomplished, the Marys proceed on their way to the sepulchre. As they walk along Marie sings:

O high king eternal
Show us this king.

Mary Jacobi cautions them that Pilate has put the sepulchre in the custody of soldiers, but Mary Salome counsels her companions that they should not fear as they are only bringing ointment to anoint their Lord. Upon this Mary Magdalen cries out, "O misery! Why is it so near to see, the death of the Redeemer?" The others join in her grief, when suddenly the Angel is before them singing that there is no need for ointment, for Christ is risen from the monument.

Behold the place!
Come, come and see.

The Marys try to realize the news as best they can. The Angel tells them neither to dread nor fear and discloses that he is the Archangel Gabriel. Thereupon he begins the initial question of the *Quem quaertis* trope—it would seem to modern taste, belatedly. At any rate the trope serves to revive the soldiers who surge forward to return to Pilate; he asks them to go home and keep silent concerning what they have seen. They bend to his will.

Mary Magdalen now stands in the left part of the church, near the sepulchre, extending her hands in prayer, and weeping sings: "*Heu! me misera.* Great has been the labor, great the grief, and great her sadness, holding in memory Jesus Christ the glory of all the world: his pity, his condoning of her grave sins, his enriching her whole life. O Master . . ." She tries to remind herself that this is a day of rejoicing but can only say that she is miserable, miserable. She can only ask the perennial questions of the grief-laden, "What can I do? What can I say?"

Suddenly Jesus is standing next to the sepulchre. He addresses Mary Magdalen: "Woman, why do you weep?"

Seeming not to recognize him, she replies: "They have killed my Lord, and I know not where they have put him."

No scene between them follows, as in the plays above, but the Angel again asks: "Quem quaeritis . . .?"

Mary Jacobi and Mary Salome answer: "The living, who was dead. A second time the Angel tells them that

He is not there; He is risen; the Son of Man traduced and crucified is gone into Gallilee.

Still unable to believe the good tidings, Mary Magdalen raises her hands in prayer to heaven: "Our Father which art in heaven, holy is thy name forever. Do not abandon me . . . O bitterness! O misery! Whom I shall inquire of or where he is I know not, Father." She falls fainting and is lifted from the ground by the other Marys, who gently remonstrate with her over-great preoccupation with the death of the Lord Jesus. She can only respond that her heart burns with desire to see him and that she asks but cannot find where he is. Granted that the repetition may be due to confusion in the manuscript, certainly the version that has come down to us is dramatic in its presentation of the obsessive grief of Mary Magdalen, creating for her a very compelling role.

Again the Archangel demands "*Quem quaeritis . . .?*" and once more reassures the Marys that there is no cause for fear but rather of rejoicing. Addressing Mary Magdalen by name he calls upon her to shout abroad that Christ is indeed risen.

There seems to be a break in the manuscript here, which is followed by a scene between Mary and the Apostle Peter, suggesting that the traditional race of Peter and John to the tomb had already been accomplished. Mary and Peter are joined by six other apostles who sing the hymn, *Jesu nostra redemcio.* All at once Jesus is among them, clothed in a dalmatica, bearing a cross in his hand: "Peace unto you. I am with you. Fear not." He shows them his hands and his feet; he is actually with them, not a spirit but palpable and visible. They gather about him, rejoicing that he is risen who for them had hung upon the cross.

Thomas comes in singing. He doubts, but when Jesus asks him to feel the place where the nail had gone into his hand, Thomas falls at the feet of his Lord crying out: "My Master and My God. Alleluia!"

Mary now moves toward the sepulchre and stands there

with the two disciples. They sing the prosa or sequence, *Victimae Paschali.* When they come to the line: "Tell us, Mary, what do you see in your path;" showing the sepulchre to them, she firmly replies that she sees the sepulchre of the living Christ and the glory of his rising. There follows the antiphon *Dux vite mortuus,* and the chorus begins "in a high voice," *Te Deum laudamus.*

Aloft into the great reaches of the Gothic cathedral would that voice ascend, falling with a sweet plenitude upon the ears of the congregation purifying and refreshing their hearts, helping them to feel even more deeply the drama of the story that they had just been witnessing. To Gustav Cohen we owe a particular debt for his realization of the importance of light to the effect of the Easter and Christmas plays.[11] The ceremony of *tenebre* on Good Friday saw the lights of the fifteen candles of a giant candelabra extinguished one by one until the church was almost in total darkness to commemorate the blotting out of the sun at the noon of Christ's crucifixion. On the other hand, the gloom of the great church was entirely lifted with an abundance of light for the Easter play, drifting down from clerestory and high rose window and fortified by such artificial means as ingenuity could devise, to create an atmosphere congruent to the effulgence of the risen Christ. As symbolic of this mood we may note the white robe of Christ in the Tours play, the dalmatica. Similarly, in Ethelwold's rubrics the Angel was vested in an alb.

But spectacle is not drama. Nor is the fact that the Tours Easter play is longer than the others significant dramatically in and of itself. That this play does uphold dramatic interest throughout its length marks it, however, as a kind of culmination in the development of the Easter play. Moreover, we see for the first time a sustained acting part in the role of Mary Magdalen, tempting the modern reader to think of her as a forerunner, though not necessarily source, of the dominant single character roles in the tragedies of Marlowe and Shakespeare. Inevitably Mary Magdalen, as written into this play by the unknown artist who composed it, presumably in some monastery cell or scriptorium, leads the mind back to the hero of Greek tragedy, to the flawed but aspiring humanity whose likeness Aristotle has defined for us as the proper hero of tragedy.

The scope of this essay will not allow a discussion of the concomitant development of the Passion Play nor of the mourning mother at the foot of the Cross in the somewhat later plays of the Virgin Mary, but they invite further study. The Christmas Play, deriving from the crèche, moves away from the development of a single dominant character. Instead of character, event controls here: the birth of King Jesus to the Immaculate Maiden. The divergence in the spring of dramatic action (even recognizing the importance of the event of the crucifixion) is all the more striking because of the almost parallel pattern of historical progression from trope to fully realized play in the Christmas as well as the Easter play. For out of the *Quem quaeritis in praesepe* trope there also grew separate plays, and these individual plays for the different days of the Christmas season were later combined into one play. Of the four of these shorter plays most often entered into such combinations: the *Officium Pastorum, Officium Stellae, Ordo Rachelis,* and *Ordo Prophetarum,* two or more might be combined as in the texts of Bilsen, Fleury, and Freising.[12] All four were joined into one long play in the *Carmina Burana* manuscript of Bebediktbeuren,[13] particularly illustrating that the force which binds all into one is the event of the miraculous birth.

There is no gainsaying that the appeal is universal; Godhead is made flesh, and the heavenly babe is born in a manger. Even the humblest peasant could respond with tenderness and grow still with awe as the Angelic host announced the event to the Shepherds, who journeyed even as later the Wise Kings from the East would do to the new king over whom the bright star loomed. Even in the *Ordo Rachelis* the event caused the action, for Herod who ordered the Slaughter of the Innocents sought thereby to exterminate this new born king. The execution of the terrible command, which presented directly the killing of the Innocents by the soldiers, threw to the winds the Greek restraint against violent action on stage but used a procedure, it must be confessed, still existent in modern drama. Even the grim Medieval touch in the justice meted out to Herod, who was eaten by "worms" emphasized the horror at the infanticide. The *Ordo Prophetarum* was doctrinal, bringing forward evidence from Daniel, Isaiah, and other Prophets, including the Sibyl from classical lore, and Vergil with whom to certify belief in the birth of the Son of God to the Virgin, the lily flower. In the Bebediktbeuren play, the doctrine comes as a relief from the shudder invoked by the Massacre. The unknown writer of this play endowed it with a special dignity in that the rubric called for a seat for Augustine "in fronte ecclesie". For the first time the great churchman moderated the debate concerning the birth to a Maiden unknown by any man, who with her purity cleansed the world of sin. Flanked on his right by the Prophets, Augustine leads the verbal battle with the Archisynogogus and his Sycophants at the left. Ultimately Augustine and his forces overwhelm their doubting opponents. The glory is once more re-established. In this version the prophecy of Virgil is invoked by the half-mad Sibyl who moves inconstantly about beneath the Star of Bethlehem hung high above. But in the thirteenth century *Prophetae* from Laon[14] Virgil is represented in person, described in the Order of Prophets as "Virgil, with an ink-horn and candle-stick, crowned with ivy, holding a quill pen," ready to voice his prophecy from the Fourth Eclogue that a heavenly babe born of a Virgin would usher in a new golden age.

The Christmas plays were given at and represent a time of rejoicing and gift-giving. Appropriately it was the event represented by the crèche that set the great cathedrals again ablaze with light, ringing with song. But Augustine and Virgil notwithstanding, the Christmas plays held no role dramatically comparable to Mary Magdalen's in the Tours Easter play.

Notes

[1]J. Q. Adams, *Chief Pre-Shakespearean Dramas,* Boston, 1924, 3; E. K. Chambers, *The Mediaeval Stage,* 2 vols., Oxford, 1903, II, 9. See also Karl Young, *The Drama of the Medieval Church,* 2 vols., Oxford, 1933, I, 204-5. My debt to the fine scholarship of Young demands special acknowledgement, here, and throughout.

[2]Gustave Cohen, *Histoire de la mise en scène dans le théatre religieux francaise du moyen age,* Paris, 1951, 27-29; Chambers, II, 41; Young, 9-11.

[3]J. M. Manly, *Specimens of Pre-Shakespearean Drama,* 2 vols. completed, London 1897, I, v. See also Jean Bony, *French Cathedrals,* London, 1951, (2nd. ed., 1954), 5 and *passim.*

[4]Chambers, II, 14, 15.

[5]Young, I, 229.

[6]*Ibid.* I, 239.

[7]*Ibid.,* I, 412-447.

[8]Compare *Coriolanus,* I, i, 1st Citizen, 2nd Citizen; I, iv, 1st Soldier, 2nd Soldier, etc. II, ii; II, iii; IV, v; IV, vi; V, ii; V, v; V, vi. and also *Timon of Athens* and *Henry VIII* as evidencing the continuation of numerical designation of character in Shakespeare.

[9]I, 447.

[10]Chambers, II, 42.

[11]18, 19; 32.

[12]Young, II, 172; Chambers, II, 44-52; Cohen, 20.

[13]Munich, Staatsbibliothek MSlat 4660 fol. 99^{r}-104^{v}, reprinted in Young, II, 172-190.

[14]Adams, 41-48.

W. L. Halstead

Artifice In Sir Gawain

A *friend and colleague,* Professor Fred Shaw, has said that he reads *Sir Gawain and the Green Knight* every year just to see if *this time* Sir Gawain gives in to the Lady. The idea startled me, and I guiltily wondered if my own frequent returns to the story were for the same reprehensible reason. But then I defend myself and friend Shaw with the thought that neither of us will probably return to *Peyton Place.*[1] In *Sir Gawain* it is not the content itself but the skill of the presentation that has entrapped us, probably for the rest of our lives. I still wonder what makes me re-read the story time after time. Probably it is for the same reason that the author's admirers thought enough of the poem to want it recorded in such an expensive manuscript as MS. Nero A. x.[2]

Aside from the puzzlement of how Sir Gawain resists a beautiful lady sitting on the side of his bed in the refreshing hours of a winter morning, there are many questions in connection with the poem. What had the fall of Troy to do with a chivalric story that evidently engrossed people sometime between 1200 and 1400 A. D.? Of course, Dares Phrygius and Dictys Cretensis[3] had Latinized and popularized the Troy story, and the early chroniclers[4] had connected the British with the last of the Trojans. The English are a stubborn people and have been insisting for several hundred years that they did not descend from trees, and a re-assuring reminder of a respectable ancestry did not detract from the appeal of *Sir Gawain*, the materials of which were right in the line of descent from Troy.

There is not much question about the motivation with which the author began his main story. Everyone knows that in one of the analogues to the story King Arthur could not eat until his digestive apparatus was excited by a marvelous story or deed. Arthur, in history or legend, did not starve to death, and so our *Gawain* poet had sufficient reason to introduce the Green Knight and the beheading. Beheading before an audience has appealed since, all the way through Elizabethan drama to modern vaudeville. And the problem has always been the same: how construct the body to be decapitated? In reading *Sir Gawain*, one has to wait for the answer until the end of the poem which is not, because of other interests, too long. The *Gawain* poet knew how to keep people waiting.

Waiting a whole year to see how Gawain kept his head and the Knight lost his might get tiresome were it not for the fact that in the meantime we enjoy spring, get a "build-up" during the English summer, pleasure in the fruits of autumn, but dread the rigors and trials of approaching winter. What a time for a real ordeal of submitting to having one's head chopped off! One looks forward to winter and the prospective head chopping with some trepidation, to say the least. There might be something of a pleasant and exciting time introduced along about Christmas. Whoever had a proffered Christmas present such as was offered Gawain! How would you like to wake up one wintery morning to find a beautiful lady sitting on the side of your bed with intentions of heavens knows what? Most of us, being fairly decent fellows, would do some fancy mental footwork, like Sir Gawain. I have never quite figured out how Sir Gawain brings it off. The Poet was a bit beyond his depth or ambiguously clever at this point. Gawain saved himself, how I do not know[5] but he did, and more power to him. What he took each time from the Lady was little enough to exchange for a deer, a boar, and a fox.

In those days, there must have been important people interested in how to catch and butcher deer, boars, and foxes. It all happened at the same time that the Lady was sitting on the side of Gawain's bed. But there have always been the types who have preferred hunting. Also, there have always been a lot of good fellows who would not quite know what to do about a lady sitting on the side of the bed, since by all tradition and accepted mores the male should be in pursuit, or else something is wrong. (Much later, even Romeo felt this when he accidentally overheard Juliet's declaration.) Gawain was no fool. Something was wrong with the pattern of things, and he did exactly right. He dallied, with words, for time. And it all goes to show that one should not lose his head in the most trying of situations.

In the obvious there is always more than meets the eye. Not only was Gawain chaste, courteous, and virtuous; he was shrewd.[6] There was more than natural inclinations on the part of a lady who would come to sit on the side of a stranger's bed (three times) in a cold castle in the middle of the winter. Besides, Gawain, a man of his word, was pledged to exchange whatever he received for the catch of the man of the house on a hunt. There were technical difficulties involved. Turning in the kisses for the hunting catches was no great problem, not even embarrassing as it might be in the Twentieth Century, especially in America. It would pass unnoticed in Italy and France.

That bedroom business was a bit tight, and so we are almost glad to get out into the fresh, biting atmosphere of the Green Chapel, wherever it was.[7] That girdle business was a bit thick, but what was a mere girdle in a situation involving one's head! A man might grasp at a girdle as well as at a straw. There might be more to girdles than meets the eye, and the man of the house might never miss the girdle. Proper respect for a girdle might save a man's life.[8] It was all a strange affair anyway. A man ought to take something from a lady sitting on the side of his bed in the glow of a winter's morning.[9]

Bercilak's three feints at Gawain's neck make us all cringe, and we understand Gawain perfectly at this point. There is another point. Aside from wondering at each reading if, this time, the Lady will not simply sit on the side of the bed, suppose, this time, Bercilak is nervous and his control is not so good. Have we all been waiting these many years for Gawain's head to roll down the mound crowned by the Green Chapel?

At the end, the explanation of the whole business is not hard to accept. A person like Gunievere ought to have been taken down a bit (by 1350 everyone knew about her), and a down to earth woman like Morgan la Fay, who had learned some tricks from Merlin, was just the person to do it. The first beheading really wasn't much of a trick. Even in the Twentieth Century, with a bit of framework and cloth, we can construct a figure that can stand beheading. At the same time a young untried relative (Gawain) might be made look good to an assembly of peers who had made careers of trying to look good in a time that had high standards for such achievement.

At the close, we are back to Troy again. Don't ask me why, except that is where we started, and a man who could write *Sir Gawain* ought to show that he knew a few things about the world. A reliable background like the history of the world since the fall of Troy could well include something like Gawain's strange adventure, and the people who followed *Sir Gawain* were again assured that they had not come down out of trees and were back in good solid history where they had placed themselves with the help of Nennius and Geoffrey of Monmouth.[10]

The foregoing Introduction is offered as evidence that

the *Sir Gawain* Poet was, above all, a Literary Artist. That is to say that he knew beforehand the condition and degree of receptivity he wanted to achieve, and he knew the artistic and artifice devices to use.

Scholarship has looked for evidence of an anthropologist, a historian, a preacher, a philosopher, and several other varieties of the creative poet with a message.[11] The fact is that there is probably everything in the poem that interpreters have found, but the single critic should not attempt to elbow all the others out of the picture. There is good probability that the *Gawain* Poet had no single didactic purpose but was content to have any and all deductions that could be made by his clientele. Lively debate following a related story could have been a parlour game of the time, the same as it was in the later novelle and the courtly romances of Castioglione, Gascoigne, Sidney, and Lyly.

The known and hypothetical old analogues of *Sir Gawain*[12] may have each been didactic in its particular way and substance, and the wraiths of myth and legend may well haunt our masterpiece, bitter at cavalier treatment, each vying for recognition but nearly obscured by other Shades in competition for substantive form.

The Gawain Poet was a conscious literary artist intent upon an effective story. He was not a prophet or historian. He was adequate in talent and skill to the extent of the demands of his task. He integrated techniques, devices, and artistic methods in unified structure to a degree nowhere apparent in extant metrical romances. As a literary artist, master of techniques, he belongs in the company of Poe, O. Henry, and Maupassant.

Our Poet rang the changes on the interests of his clientele and played on credibility with sure-fire devices.

The use of archaic alliterative verse was aimed at conservative aristocrats looking back toward literature of a respected antiquity, while the quatrain rhymes of the Wheel-and-Bob stanza appealed to ears newly attuned to courtly French musical importation. The natively old was integrated with a rising vogue in new poetry. Presented with such appeal in the verse and stanza, everyone could be made receptive to the vehicle for the story.

The seige of Troy introductory material worked in three ways: afforded satisfaction in reviving pleasurable associations with previous literary experiences, catered to the English grasp for a respectable ancestry, and linked the Arthurian material securely in the chain of legendary Western Civilization, to overcome fragmentary disorder and layered confusion in surviving Arthurian epos. The Gawain Poet did not borrow or build on sources but cut through, hewed away, then put together in a complete rewriting to make an artistic structure. His story is in a straight line in a chronology extending back to Troy, an episode or short story in a background master plot.

His episode needed its own introduction in the setting of the Christmas festival at Camelot with its conventional appeals in images of luxury, leisure, and play. This too was aimed at revival of story experiences, a basic, universal pleasure of recall and recognition.

Thus the stage was set, and the story followed a basic structural pattern of Preparation, Motivation, Initial Incident, Sustaining Substance and Devices, a Main Climax, and the Conclusion.

"Preparation" was provided with the anticipatory atmosphere and expectancy in the assembly at Camelot. Motivation for the Initial Incident, Arthur's insistence on an adventure, was taken from a source. Anticipation was fulfilled and interest heightened with the Initial Incident of the plot—the weird knight, the strange bargain, and the exciting beheading.

The raconteur adopted the reliable over-all sustaining device of Delayed Explanation. A year would pass before any of us, Arthur's court, the Poet's contemporaries, and we later readers, would know the why and how of what had happened. He who resorts to Delayed Explanation must provide immediate interests to fill the time gap. The extended lyric of the seasons served both as diversion and for illusion of slow passing of time until the time for the quest for the Green Chapel. The quest was a conventional story-frame device familiar to the age of romances.

Sir Gawain's quest was given all the usual preparations and rigors of journey. Versimilitude was heightened with geographical references. Instead of combat encounters, a second story, the Temptations at the castle, was used, affording all the elements of another well constructed plot. Our poet's mastery of plotting devices is illustrated by his use of "Three-in-Series" climaxes—three temptations, three kisses, three exchanges, three days of hunting with catches of three different animals. The Gawain Poet knew the value of climax within climax.

At the Green Chapel we have the three-in-series again to build to the main climax in the three feints with the axe toward Gawain's bared neck. The slight nick of the flesh has its obvious philosophical explanation as atonement for Gawain's slight and human imperfection — harmless deception to preserve life.

At last we have an end to the long sustaining device of Delayed Explanation. By legerdemain, Morgan la Fay had contrived the Green Knight and all that followed.

The conclusion is a recall to the original physical setting and a replacement of the immediate story in the illusionary chain of legendary history starting with the fall of Troy.

The mechanical structure of *Sir Gawain* is a work of art in kind. The *Gawain* Poet knew how to construct a story, and, in retrospect, his conscious artistry is apparent. His workmanship in story substance is of equal quality, but there is not space here for detailed analysis or repetition of excellent studies already at hand in editions and periodicals. One instance, however, is remarkable and worthy of note. Our Poet knew the artistic use of ambiguity, something that has had a recent vogue as a discovery in modern criticism.[13] I point to Gawain's desperate juggling of wordy logic to dissuade the persistent Lady. Several times I have tried to follow Gawain's argumentative

(?), persuasive (?) chain of thought. I am convinced that his position is secure without his or the Lady's embarrassment, but I cannot make out the reasons. I am sure that the situation was vitally handled in the plotting. The effect is realistically accomplished. Since no real passion on the part of the Lady was at stake, she withdrew each time from the bedchamber in mental confusion.

Our Poet was a rewriter of materials with artistic intent. He aimed at getting all reactions possible from a total structure of art, and anyone (then or now) can have his own ideational, imagistic, aesthetic, historical, philosophical, religious, etc. experiences as reactions to this work of art, and therein lies the value of *Sir Gawain and the Green Knight.*

Notes

[1]A novel of the 1950's that left nothing to be anticipated and little to be imagined.

[2]I have not seen the MS., but it must have been expensive.

[3]I have not seen these works, either, but everyone drops the names casually.

[4]I have seen the edited chronicles.

[5]See if you can figure out what Sir Gawain said to satisfy the Lady without offense.

[6]This is not a good term to apply to a nearly perfect knght; perhaps it would be better to say Gawain was knowledgeable.

[7]Everybody, then and since, has had fun trying to locate it (the Green Chapel).

[8]And probably has.

[9]I don't know why I keep insisting on the weather.

[10]A couple of chroniclers who knew a lot about "making" history.

[11]The *Sir Gawain* field of study, accomplished work and potentialities, has been well presented by Morton W. Bloomfield, "*Sir Gawain and the Green Knight*: An Appraisal," PMLA, LXXVI, No. 1, March 1961, pp. 7-19.

[12]See INTRODUCTION and NOTES, *Sir Gawain & the Green Knight,* edited by J. R. R. Tolkien and E. V. Gordon, Clarendon Press, 1925, corrected impression 1930.

[13]See Mr. Empson's *Seven Types of Ambiguity.*

John I. McCollum, Jr.

The House of Fame Revisited

Students have found that THE HOUSE OF FAME lends itself to numerous and rather varied interpretations, the results of which have left interpretative criticism concerning the work in a somewhat unsettled state. So ingenious have been the hypotheses that it would seem that a new poem has been created from inferential analyses. W. O. Sypherd was thus led to remind us that the poem should be interpreted not by reading between the lines but by reading the lines themselves.[1] This is not to say that such speculation and theorizing have no value, for assuredly they may serve to point out the richness of the poem, and in so doing lead to a greater appreciation of the poet's genius. This *is* to say that our failures to understand may be the result of our refusal to read the lines for what they contain rather than for what our theories demand that they contain.

Inevitably the critics have found autobiographical, allegorical, or occasional significance in the poem. Aage Brusendorff holds that the poet intended to celebrate the marriage of Richard II and Anne of Bohemia.[2] Frederick

C. Riedel concludes that the poem was written as a rebuke referring to John of Gaunt's relations with women and to his ill-advised appearance in public with his mistress, Katherine Swynford, coincident with a long period of unpopularity resulting from the Duke's military failures, suspected designs on the English throne, and Castilian marriage which appeared to involve international difficulties.[3]

Emile Legouis feels that the poem was written for no special occasion and that the poet had no definite aim at first. It is, rather, an attempt in a humorous way to re-tell Dante, not by parody but by a simple re-casting of the poetry in a lower key.[4]

One of the most detailed considerations is that of W. O. Sypherd's Chaucer Society study. Here the poem is classified as "a love-vision of the literary *genre* to which belong such poems as *Le Roman de la Rose,* Froissart's *Paradys d' Amours* and Chaucer's *Duchesse.*" Chaucer's purpose, Sypherd suggests, was to write a dream poem on the subject of love, expressing, in so doing, a feeling for the realities of experience so well portrayed in the later poems. Rejecting the possibility that the fame material suggested the poem, he proposes, instead, that Chaucer was primarily interested in the worship of love, a subject interesting to his contemporaries, and concludes that the poem is "absolutely complete within itself [save for the necessarily brief missing conclusion] and that it has no other purpose than that which is more than once definitely expressed in the words of Chaucer himself."[5]

Paull F. Baum writes that Chaucer must have begun with the idea of a lightly handled, even facetious, poem on Fame in the manner of the French love-visions. He concludes that relatively little of the poem is lost and that the missing portion contains no news or announcement of great importance. The poet returns to his books with the conclusion that in love, if not in all of life, the poetic dream is preferable to earthly reality.[6]

J. M. Manly rejects the allegorical interpretations and argues that the poem as it now stands is but a prologue and that the "newe tydynges" are to be revealed in a group of tales. Such a plan, he decides, must have been abandoned in favor of a greater project, *The Canterbury Tales.*[7] A similar theory was advanced by R. C. Goffin,[8] who equates the word *tidings* with *stories*: the poet's reward for his services to love's folk, therefore, was to be in the form of new stories.

Bertrand H. Bronson dismisses the personal idealistic allegory theory and argues that the poem is no mere prologue to a group of love tales but is nearly complete as it stands, lacking only the conclusion and thus the climax. That climax, he suggests, without offering a candidate, was to be a revelation of some gossip, perhaps of a great man's infidelity in love.[9]

This summary does not exhaust by any means the suggestions that have been set forth in an attempt to determine the poet's meaning. In general there has been no satisfactory resolution of the critical debate. While many of the hypotheses have an incidental interest and suggest intriguing avenues for speculation, they do not clarify the basic issues. It is the purpose of this essay to reconsider the poem without the benefit of a specific hypothesis in the hope that Chaucer may have been clear enough in developing his thesis to lead us to a reasonable conclusion.

There seems to be little doubt that the poem demonstrates some mastery of technique, characteristic of his later work. The elaborately emphasized rhetoric of the proems and invocations, the obvious parody of the epic manner, and the persistent intermingling of the humorous and serious make it impossible for the reader not to anticipate the poet's later handling of *Troilus and Criseyde* and *The Canterbury Tales.*

Scholars, in general, have agreed that the work was written probably between 1379, immediately after Chaucer's second trip to Italy, and 1384, before his relinquishment of the appointment to the Customs Office. Most scholars feel that it preceded *Troilus and Criseyde* and that it is transitional in nature, being in structure a love-vision and in treatment a demonstration of his interest in the classical Latin and contemporary Italian literature. The individualistic treatment of borrowed materials gives the piece a peculiar attractiveness that was to become characteristic of the later poems.

The three-book division advanced by Caxton and Thynne does not seem balanced from the standpoint of the number of lines nor from the standpoint of subject matter. Baum has suggested that the work might more properly contain four divisions (the additional division occurring at line 778 of Book III, thus according to the fourth division 290 lines and what he feels to be a missing conclusion). This arrangement, practical as it may appear, does not seem to have been considered by Chaucer in view of the specific invocational elements to the second and third portions and the reference at line 1093 to the "lytel laste bok." Despite Chaucer's apparent neglect, the balance of the poem certainly suggests the propriety of adjustment.

Despite the long inner digressions concerning the nature of sound and the descriptions of the palace of the goddess Fame, the work is essentially devoted to the poet's hope to hear tidings—of what he is not sure, possibly of love and of love's folk. All the major elements of the poem are directed to that end.

The poem opens with a vigorous and subtly humorous commentary on the subject of dreams, the conclusion of which is that the author knows nothing about the subject and that he does not care to tax his wits with the problem. Such affairs he is willing to leave to clerks who "trete of this and other werkes." The commentary is occasioned by his having experienced a remarkable dream which he proposes to relate, the significance of which, however, he does not understand. Praying repetitiously that God "turne us every drem to goode," he amusingly invokes the blessing of the god of sleep, "yf every drem stonde in his might," and asks God to give joy to those who hear the dream well and scorn it not. To those who misjudge it through perversity, he adds, "... every harm that any man/Hath had, syth the world began,/ Befalle hym thereof ..."[10]

Having disposed of his friends and critics, he commences the narrative of the wonderful dream. On the night of December 10 he, while dreaming, found himself in a temple of glass dedicated to the goddess of Love. On the walls he found portrayed in a series of scenes an epitome of the story of the *Aeneid.* In keeping with the character of the temple, and incidentally the character of the dream-poem, the portrayal concentrates upon the love affair between Aeneas and Dido, and emphasizes, as did the original, the part played by Venus; this story in the dreamer's mind becomes a love tiding. Chaucer concludes his account of Dido's unhappy affair with her lament on the general unfaithfulness of men and the particular deceit of Aeneas and with the bitter reflection that shame will incur to her name when the history of her act is "red and songe/Over al thys lond, on every tonge." Her complaint ends with an address to "wikke Fame," through whom every hidden thing is known. The account is then interrupted by the poet with a reflection on "the harm, the routhe" that result from "untrouthe."

This introductory book of the poem is devoted primarily to love, with some retention from the source of the influence of the goddess in behalf of her votaries; incidental to the element of love, Chaucer utilizes a suggestion of the Rumor-Fame personification, also a part of his source *(Aeneid,* Bk. IV, ll. 174ff.). Despite the fact that this is Aeneas's story, the reader is impressed by Chaucer's emphasis on Dido's position and by his ultimate focus on Fame as a shaming and punitive power. Dido, acknowledging that men love for only three reasons—fame, friendship, and pleasure—can, for having "loved al to sone a gest," expect only shame, dealt by the revealing nature of Fame.

This then is a story of tragic love, as Baum points out. The reader may note that the poet excerpts the love episode from the greater story; that while he is aware of the deceit of Aeneas, he emphasizes the foolishness of

Dido and is willing to "excusen Eneas/Fullyche of al his grete trespas"; that he requires Dido to recognize the shame that will accrue to her name as a result of her having loved unwisely; and that the detailed narration concludes with a reflection on the power of Fame or Rumor. Having introduced these matters, the poet then prepares to lead his reader into the realm of actual experience.[11] As to the ultimate conclusion of his direction critical opinion diverges. It is possible that his narration leads to a rejection of the love-vision form; or, more likely, he is leading us to the not so dramatic quest for love tidings, of which the Aeneas-Dido story is a prime example; or, simply to our adventure with Fame or Rumor, which may relate to tidings or rumors of love affairs and their ramifications.

Upon leaving the temple, the poet finds himself in a desert where he saw "no maner creature/That ys yformed be Nature," who might advise or instruct him concerning his whereabouts. Impressed by the desolation, he prays that Christ protect him from "fantome and illusion." Casting his eyes heavenward in the act of prayer, he is suddenly aware of a golden eagle, more wonderful than any ever before seen by man. The transition to the second adventure begins.

That the desert has allegorical or symbolical significance, as many scholars seem to require, is a possibility. It may represent the barrenness of life separated from love, and/or it may represent the sense of literary desolation caused by an abandonment of the unsatisfactory love-vision form. There seems to be little in the text to support such hypotheses, however.[12] In view of the eagle's description, the ivory tower more appropriately represents the poet's situation than does the desert. The eagle admits that the poet suffers "debonairly" while the desert concept requires that he recognize his barrenness. In another sense the symbol, thus interpreted, fails: the desert is utterly desolate; the dreamer is lost and needs a guide—a condition which he recognizes and seeks to remedy. He does not recognize that need in his life nor is there evidence that he seeks guidance in his daily affairs. Even in the desert he is not without recourse. He, like Aeneas and as the dreamer, is a wanderer and is being led by the exigency of the dream, he knows not where. We might assume that had not the eagle appeared the dreamer could have returned to the temple and to the care of Venus, about whom he had just commented. The scene, therefore, stands more acceptably as a literary transition piece designed to isolate the character from one experience in order to introduce him into another. He leaves the temple of his own will to seek information, not about love but about his surroundings.[13] The desert scene actually gives the dream element of Chaucer's treatment more reality, for such appearances are in the nature of dreams. Admittedly the reality of the situation does not negate the symbolism. The end of the story, what we have of it, does not indicate that the poet was necessarily more attuned to the affairs of the world or that he was less barren; if anything, he was more satisfied to return to his books, or he had been converted into a gossip-monger.

The invocation to Book II retains the suggestion that the goddess of Love might influence the action. In this book, however, the action is transferred more specifically to the dreamer himself. Accompanying his appeal to Venus by a prayer to the Muses and to his own Thought, he resumes his description of the eagle and the action appertaining.

The poet is roused from his fright by the eagle's assurance that he would suffer no harm and that "this caas" was for his "lore" and "prow." The illusions and fantasies about which he had prayed now beset him temporarily. The eagle explains at length that the dreamer is not to be "stellyfyed" although he is assuredly under the control of Jupiter, who pities the poet because he has served truly and devotedly Cupid and Venus without recompense or reward. So intense has been the poet's devotion to his books that he has received no tidings of love or of love's folk, nor of anything else in life—he hears nothing of the world. Jupiter, therefore, through his grace and in recompense for the dreamer's devotion, has decreed that he is to be carried to the House of Fame, where he is to hear wondrous things and tidings of love, both true and untrue, and through his own observation discover those things about which he has hitherto been satisfied only to read.

The dreamer's incredulity gives the loquacious eagle opportunity to demonstrate his intellectual powers in a lengthy discussion of the theory of sound. While his guide proudly displays his learning, the poet finds himself reverting mentally to his books when the speaker indulges in a discussion of astronomical and geographical wonders. Upon the eagle's offer to expound at length, the passenger protests that he is too old to learn and is content to depend upon his books and "hem that write of this matere." After a time they see before them the House of Fame, from whence issues a "grete soun . . . that rumbleth up and doun." Book II ends with a short statement from the guide upon the personification of the sounds and with the eagle's prayer that "God of heven sende the grace/Some good to lernen in this place."

As in the case of the desert passage, the flight of the eagle lends itself to allegorical interpretation. It may represent the rejection of book knowledge in favor of actual experience. Of course the entire trip is for the purpose of seeing and hearing what he had heretofore only read, and the eagle refers to proof by "experience" twice (ll. 788, 878). On the whole, it would seem that if the flight represents in any way a quest for actual experience as opposed to second-hand knowledge, it is not successful. It does function to suggest the passage of time and the traversal of distance; moreover it provides a means of relaying information concerning the poet, his involvement in such an affair, and the nature of coming experiences. Surprisingly enough, neither the dreamer nor the eagle refers to the Temple of Venus and its relationship to the adventure as a whole.

Chaucer allows his dreamer a momentary reflection on his books because such a reaction would be entirely natural to one so devoted to learning: here was an opportunity to validate or disprove the assumptions of the authors to whom he had devoted his time. His rejection of the eagle's offer to discourse more fully on the subject of the stars did not constitute a denial of the validity of experiential knowledge; it was more specifically a rejection of the eagle's propensity for lengthy elucidation. When the dreamer had a question, as in the case of the movement of sound and the embodiment of rumor, he did not hesitate to ask for information.

In preparing to relate the events concerning his experience in the palace of Fame, the dreamer invokes Apollo's guidance. The account of the dream continues with the poet's ascension of the mountain of ice, on the sides of which are recorded the names of famous people. The names on the south side of the mountain are in process of deterioration, "so unfamous was woxe hir fame." Those on the north side in the shadow of the palace were as fresh as they were on the day they were inscribed. The architecture of the palace was beyond description; the appointments were exceedingly lavish; the splendor of all that he gazed upon dazzled him. In various niches were memorials of fame's servants. In the palace were harpers, minstrels, musicians, jugglers, sorcerers, and magicians—all famous personages and all purveyors of fame. Placed about the hall were statues of the great historians of antiquity, and in the company were many who had "writen olde gestes," so numerous that it would be confusing to hear all the stories or even the names of the writers. In the midst of all he saw enthroned the goddess who grew and diminished as he watched.

Fortunately she was granting audience to her petitioners; the dreamer was thus given the opportunity to observe the indiscriminate handling of appeals for fame. After nine companies had been heard, the poet was approached by a stranger, who inquired whether or not he too had come seeking fame, to whom he wisely replied that he had not so come, and as far as that matter was concerned, he would be content to take his chances as they presented themselves. In answer to a second question, he announces that he had come to learn "somme newe tydings," what tidings he did not know. His object was simply "tydynges, other this or that,/Of love, or suche thynges glade." He adds that he has not found what he wanted thus far, for "these be no suche tydynges/As I mene of."

The stranger then offers to lead him to the House of Rumor, where he would assuredly hear what he wanted. This strange place was never at rest and always filled with tidings, sometimes loud, sometimes whispered, of war, peace, marriages, love, hate, and all the other affairs of mankind. His interest aroused, he takes the initiative for the first time, and requests the eagle to await his investigation. The eagle acquiesces, for his instructions had been to further with all his might the poet's acquisition of tidings, and in the House of Rumor he will "anoon many oon lere." With the eagle's assistance he enters and begins immediately to rush about seeking information. Everywhere he hears tidings; he discovers the process by which a rumor grows and gradually changes its nature; he notes that many tidings are actually compounded of both truth and falsehood and that all tidings, when ready to be sent into the world, repair to the goddess Fame for proper dispensation.

In the house were shipmen, pardoners, couriers, and messengers—all with bags and boxes full of lies. Moving about rapidly, the poet comes upon a tiding from a foreign country, with which he teases his reader. Finally his attention was attracted to a corner of the hall where men told of love-tidings. So eager were they to hear, that members of the company jumped over one another, trod upon each other, and created a general furor. Suddenly the poet saw a man whom he could not name but who obviously was a person of great authority. Here the poem breaks off—by accident or intent.

While much of Book III is devoted to the House of Fame and while the poet prays in the invocation for power to describe the House of Fame, his objective really seems to have been the House of Rumor, for it is here that he received the type of tidings promised by the eagle. Book III and the poem seem only incidentally concerned with Fame as Renown, despite the digressive attention devoted to it. It is peculiar that while the eagle seems to have been in possession of all the facts concerning the journey, he never mentions the House of Rumor and promises that the poet will be amused and diverted in the House of Fame. One cannot but wonder what occurred while Chaucer was writing the poem. It seems not impossible that this is actually an unfinished and unrevised work. Of course such speculation leads us nowhere. Is it probable that Chaucer became aware of the two aspects of his goddess only after he had completed Book II? All that he had attributed to the House of Fame in Book II appears in the House of Rumor in Book III; the evidence, in the light of Chaucer's practice in other works, seems to point to lack of revision. The material remains the same; the source of the tidings is simply changed.

Conjectures relative to the man of authority are numerous. Many scholars have identified him with Richard II, from whom Chaucer hoped to receive patronage. Riedel identifies him with John of Gaunt. Most authorities agree that some announcement is to be made. However, it is more probable that no statement of great importance is to be made from the House of Rumor, which is filled not only with truth, but with lies, and truth compounded with lies. The dreamer himself does not indicate a willingness to reveal anything of a definite nature; in fact, he refuses to do so on one occasion. The most that the man of authority could do under such conditions would be to bring the poem to a close. In a dream context, such a device for an abrupt conclusion is not ineffective; Caxton's reasoning, therefore, may not be far afield.

The man of "gret auctorite" may bear further scrutiny. By definition he would have command; his appearance at this juncture may imply the intention of a command, either in connection with the dreamer's life or with the dream itself. The poem does not prepare us adequately for a command relative to a change in the poet's literary habits, nor is the autobiographical element developed fully enough to merit a command concerning the poet's life relative to worldly affairs. While the eagle, acting at the command of Jupiter, comments on certain aspects of the poet's life, there is no indication that the purpose of the journey is anything more than a search for tidings of this and that. We may reasonably assume that the man of authority will do or say little that will interfere with the normal course of the poet's life. A command to relate the dream could hardly be useful here, inasmuch as the significance of the dream is unclear. In this light, the narrator's comment on the mystery of dreams and his reiterated prayer "God turne us every drem to goode" acquire more meaning.

Whatever it was that the dreamer was to learn, he had not learned at the time of his entrance into the House of Rumor, if that learning was to be of a positive nature. It appears that he rejected what possibilities the eagle's disquisitions or the experience in the House of Fame may have offered. When he requested the eagle to await his quest in the House of Rumor, he spoke in this wise: "Y preye the/That thou a while abide me,/For Goddis love, and lete me seen/What wondres in this place been;/For yit, paraunter, y may lere/Som good thereon, or sumwhat here/That leef me were, or that y wente." He has not lost hope; he may yet learn or hear something which will attract him. It may be noted, however, that what was to be learned apparently must be discovered by the poet, not intentionally revealed by Jove, the eagle, or some other power. Further, the poet's references to the *good* to be learned are always broad—suggesting that he is merely to learn tidings of something undefined or of a general nature, possibly but not necessarily of love, rather than some specific tiding. The value of the tidings apparently will be determined not by Jupiter but by the poet.

In a positive way from the House of Fame he learned where the goddess dwelt, her description, her nature, and the order and process of her judgments. He knew already that some folk diversely desired fame, praise, and reputation. In a negative sense he learned that it would be wise for him to trust to his own capacities rather than to seek the bounty of the capricious goddess. He actually rejects the possible reward of fame or renown. He certainly learned very little about life, and while he may have heard stories, they did not impress him enough to require re-telling.

Despite the attempts of the learned eagle to instruct the discomfited poet while en route to the palace of Fame, his efforts are positively rejected or at best passively received. The general result of the eagle's efforts is negative; the poet is still confident that his books can supply his need.

It would seem, therefore, that if the dreamer learned anything specific from his wonderful dream such knowledge must have come from the House of Rumor, where he found a whirling mass of gossip, lies, and compounded truth. The situation aroused some interest. Again, in a positive sense, he discovered the nature of the house; he observed the dissemination of tidings; he noted how many tidings arrive; he must have learned some tidings that interested him enough to arouse a teasing comment. In a negative sense, he may have learned the compromising nature of such information and the unstable basis for much that is passed for truth.

Most scholars speculating on the question feel that the knowledge gained was primarily of a negative nature. Baum, for example, suggests that the poet learns that all fame is travesty, that renown is a mockery. He returns to his books more convinced of their validity in contrast to the farcical nature of the earthly experience.[14] Emile Legouis, on the other hand, feels that the poet concluded that he was unsuited for exalted literary endeavor: the poem "voices Chaucer's decided refusal to surrender himself completely to the sublime, or to believe deeply in the pure conception of the spirit."[15]

Perhaps the dreamer was not yet conscious of a positive conclusion that might be transferred to the mind of his audience. The opening prayer "God turne us every drem to goode" may be anticipatory. The dreamer is simply recounting in chronological sequence the details of a remarkable dream in which the revelatory power of fame and rumor is exposed. We never lose sight of the fact that the dreamer is in search of tidings; the commentary on the nature of fame and the diversity of rumor is a secondary matter which conveys to us the view that all tidings—whether they concern love or the affairs of the mundane world—originate in the House of Rumor and are capriciously disseminated by Fame. If we accept the possibility that the dreamer's search for tidings is in vain, we may be able to accept the poem as a general admonition directed at gossip and gossipers, that the poet's search for news is as foolish and as vain in the House of Rumor as it is in life, that indeed he is far better off to search for his news in books than in the deceptive world of affairs. Further expectation from the poem leads us far afield.

The poet, not understanding the nature or the significance of dreams sufficiently to offer an explanation, nevertheless, relates his experience and hopes that it may turn to good. Although the dream may have the appearance of being incomplete, it is for all practical purposes finished; nothing more of value can be had from the House of Rumor, or at least nothing we can trust. If there is a conclusion to the poem, it can serve only to bring us back to the setting with which the poem opened and perhaps Chaucer's jocular prayer that

who so thorgh presumpcion,
Or hate, or skorn, or thorgh envye,
Dispit, or jape, or vilanye,
Mysdeme hyt, pray I Jesus God
That (dreme he barefot, dreme he shod),
That every harm that any man
Hath had, syth the world began,
Befalle hym therof, or he sterve,
And graunte he mote hit ful deserve,
Lo, with such a conclusion
As had of his avision
Cresus, that was kyng of Lyde,
That high upon a gebet dyde!
This prayer shal he have of me;
I am no bet in charyte!

Notes

[1]"The Completeness of Chaucer's *Hous of Fame,*" *Modern Language Notes,* XXX (1915), 65.

[2]*The Chaucer Tradition,* London and Copenhagen, 1925, pp. 164-165.

[3]"The Meaning of Chaucer's House of Fame," *Journal of English and Germanic Philology,* XXVII (1928), 447.

[4]*Geoffrey Chaucer,* trans. L. Lailavoix, London and New York, 1913, p. 88.

[5]*Studies in Chaucer's Hous of Fame,* Chaucer Society, 2nd Series, No. 39, London, 1907, p. 65.

[6]"Chaucer's 'The House of Fame'," *Journal of English Literary History,* VIII (1941), 248-256.

[7]"What is Chaucer's *Hous of Fame?*" *Kittredge Anniversary Papers,* Boston, 1913, pp. 73-81.

[8]"Quiting By Tidings in *The Hous of Fame,*" *Medium Aevum,* XII (1943), 40-44.

[9]"Chaucer's *Hous of Fame:* Another Hypothesis," *University of California Publications in English,* III, No. 4 (1932-1944), 171-192.

[10]All citations from the text of the poem refer to *The Poetical Works of Chaucer,* ed. F. N. Robinson, Cambridge, Mass., 1933.

[11]It is tempting to speculate on the implications of the fact that the materials for the temple scene came from books, over which he had evidently sat "domb as any stoon." This phase of the dreamer's experience with its bookish fantasy suggests an interesting contrast to the more earthy relationship within the same dream with the eagle and fame.

[12]The support, if it exists, is weak. The eagle does refer to the poet's devotion to the goddess of love and to his life as paralleling that of a hermit, although his abstinence is "lyte." It would be overly subtle to force the simile in context with an anchorite withdrawn from the world in religious devotion.

[13]A. C. Garrett emphasizes the possibility of allegorical meaning. The Temple of Venus he finds to be a representation of the "peculiar interests of youth—love and its affairs." The House of Fame symbolizes the special interests of the mature life—ambition and the winning of a name. The desert "must represent a period of especial unhappiness and of doubt approaching despair; it may well stand for the dreary listlessness, the disillusion of love outgrown." ("Studies on Chancer's *House of Fame,*" *[Harvard] Studies and Notes in Philology and Literature,* Boston, 1896, V, 150-153.) Garrett's view seems to represent the over-elaboration of critics who emphasize the Dantean influence.

[14]"Chaucer's 'The House of Fame'," pp. 255-256.

[15]*Geoffrey Chaucer,* pp. 92, 97.

Jack A. Reynolds

Possible Survivals of a Matriarchal Tradition In The Literature Of The West

About *seventy years ago,* Élie Reclus, in discussing the culture of the Nairs, stated categorically, "Matrimony precedes patrimony." I should never get to the point of this paper if I belabored the general applicability of this position. In a paper this short, I cannot even indulge the luxury of a "scientific approach"—that is, I cannot present a reasonable body of evidence and then attempt to draw warranted conclusions from that evidence. I am forced rather to begin with a set of conclusions—or, more properly, hypotheses—and then examine certain exempla from the early literature of the Western world as residuals that may be best explained in terms of these hypotheses.

I shall begin with the assumption that the peoples who were the principal carriers of the Indo-European languages and cultures lived for a long period of time within the general framework of a matriarchal society, out of which gradually emerged a patriarchal society through an intervening transition period. I believe too that this matriarchy and/or the period of transition lasted much longer in the

West than we ordinarily consider and that the persistence and vigor of some of the vestigials to be examined will serve to emphasize this survival.

Very obviously, there are as many types of matriarchy that might obtain as there are types of patriarchy. To expedite matters, I must set up briefly the broad outlines of a type of matriarchy that I think was general at one time among the peoples of the West as well as certain general aspects of what I call the Transition Period.

I think we may safely disregard the romantic extremes of matriarchal concepts and assume that a truly Amazonian society was largely the result of post-facto thinking, a poorly understood social memory embellished with what the psychologist calls "projections," that is, functional and natural characteristics of a later society transferred more or less meaninglessly to an earlier and differently organized society. This applies equally well to the Greek concept of the Amazons as it does to those satiric literary works of my younger days: Robert Sherwood's play, *The Warrior's Husband* and the equally delightful and now out-moded novel, *The Coming of the Amazons.*

Allowing for flexibility of details among the various but more or less ethnically related groups of early Western man, all we need to predicate as common characteristics of the general matriarchal state are:

First, inheritance through the maternal line.

Though a more precise study of the delineation where individual groups are concerned might further elucidate some crucial points in literary exegesis, we can, for our purposes, disregard the question of whether this inheritance was shared equally by the daughters, was the full portion of the eldest, or of the youngest, or of some particular daughter selected by a system (or by mere preference) without regard to her position among the sisters. And this could apply equally well to inheritance of the chattel of nomadic tribes as well as to the somewhat different concept of "possessions" enjoyed by other groups occupying a given area of land with relative stability.

Secondly, we need to predicate fraternal authority.

In the broadest sense, fraternal authority simply means that one or more brothers exercise authority in the name of the sister.

Now such a division of social responsibility, of ownership and management, so to speak—where ownership is inherent in the female and management in the male descendents of a matriarch—though applicable to a wide variety of social customs, adapts itself most easily to a unit in which polyandry is sporadically or regularly practiced. For this implies that the social importance of the matriarch's mate or mates is virtually non-existent, once he has served the biological purpose of siring another generation.

It is really not necessary to allow for too many variations. We might instead set up a single type as fairly representative of the late matriarchy among the Indo-European peoples of the West.

Briefly, then, let us assume a social organization wherein "ownership" resided in a single daughter. I believe, for instance, that among the Celtic tribes this was generally the youngest daughter, though other tribes may have shown other preferences. And "management," or "premiership," if you prefer the term, resided in a particular brother, probably the eldest. I have reasons to believe, however, that among the Germanic tribes this management or authority was shared by several if not by all of the brothers. Furthermore, I believe that the matriarch's marital relations were probably polyandrous, if not actually casual. This type of social organization can best maintain continuity over a long period of time only if the matriarch's mate or mates have no individualized and stable claim to a position in the houshold.

You now have a household in which the two closest relationships are (a) between the mother and that particular daughter who is to replace her eventually in the mother-rôle; and (b) between the mother's brother, who performs the masculine rôle of exercising authority for her, and that particular son who will eventually replace his uncle and exercise the same authority for his own sister. A traditional pattern of apprenticeship asserts itself and makes these two very close relationships necessary: the mother necessarily training her daughter in the functions and obligations she will subsequently assume; the uncle similarly rearing and preparing his nephew to assume his responsibilities when the time comes.

Under such a system, the uncle—who is the public embodiment of authority, the gift-giver, and the arbiter of tribal justice—necessarily favors his nephew, who is in fact his heir, in all matters. And this, I suggest, is precisely what the Old Latin term we call *nepotism* originally meant, though it somewhat broadened its meaning in the more complex and sophisticated society of later days.

Under such a system, again, an intense tradition of respect for the uncle will ingrain itself in the mores of the people. In the early second century A.D. such a tradition was still so outstandingly strong among the Germanic tribes that it is given particular emphasis by Cornelius Tacitus in his *Germania.*

This does not mean that such a matriarchy still persisted in the second century A.D. among all, or even any, of those Germanic tribes whose customs Tacitus reported. Most of those tribes had probably passed well beyond even the Transition Period, but the force of tradition still dictated a powerful avuncular respect. For it is very clear from what Tacitus relates that the position of the husband was already well established.

Sociologists often speak of "cultural lag," which embraces, among other things, the persistence of attitudes and behavior patterns that were once essential to a social organization but that have become partially or completely non-functional in a later society. In short, the apparent needs of today are often overshadowed by the real needs of yesterday,—and not always to the detriment of tomorrow. To put it another way: today proposes and yesterday disposes.

At this point, we ought to consider the basic characteristics of a Transition Period, for it is in this period that the authority of the husband emerges. Inherent here is a reasonable concept and practice of monogamy; only under monogamy can the position of the husband become stabilized in the household. And once the husband emerges as a stable individual in the council of the household, he becomes a genuine threat to the position and authority of the uncle—or, more properly, his wife's brother. Eventually, of course, he replaces him. But significant and enduring social change is always "eventual." Innumerable insignificant and individual compromises, concessions, and changes are made, and ultimately must be not merely made but accepted before the pattern of the kaleidoscope is materially different. This takes time, and during that time the generalized movement is perhaps first toward the position of the husband as advisor to the dominant brother, later a partner in his authority, and finally, his replacement, with the position of the brother regressing to that of advisor before he ultimately passes out of the picture. And all during this Transition Period we may still have an essential matriarchy, provided only that the inheritance is maintained through the maternal line. And throughout this long period of change-over, even in its final stages, the position of the brother, although his authority has weakened even to the vanishing point, is still a strong one; he is traditionally revered for his wisdom, sagacity and experience.

Tacitus tells us that was still the position of the brother, or what he calls the uncles, among the Germanic tribes he describes. To quote him more precisely:

> The uncle on the mother's side regards his nephews with an affection not at all inferior to that of their father. With some the relation of the sister's children to their maternal uncle is held to be the strongest tie of consanguinity . . .

I said that Tacitus tells "us"; as a matter of fact he wasn't telling us at all; he was telling his fellow Romans. I think we are too inclined today to regard Tacitus as something between a mere journalistic reporter on the one hand and a dispassionate and objective early social scientist on the other. This, I believe, is to misread Tacitus; there is a satiric and almost cruel didacticism throughout the

Germania, mitigated by an underlying noble and moralistic tone. Briefly, he is reminding the Romans that the salt of the earth has lost some of its savor. The objectivity of his report is only apparent; to sophisticated Roman readers it must have been quite evident that the forest-dwelling savage beyond the Rhine had preserved certain homely virtues (despite his generally uncultivated and illiterate condition) that the noble Roman, that darling of the Gods, had abandoned to his detriment. Just one of these virtuous lapses happened to be the high respect for the uncles—we today may or may not consider that a serious loss in itself —but what is significant is that the loss, that is, of a powerful vestigial of a matriarchate, had been sufficiently recent that Tacitus could mourn that loss.

It is evident that social man has no better memory than individual man. The social satirist often performs for society the same function that the psychiatrist or, more traditionally, the priest performs for individual man: he frees us of our guilt in the present by having us remember and understand the past.

About six hundred years before Tacitus, the Greeks had a much closer perspective and understanding of this social order—the order of the Transition Period—and represented it in their literature from time to time with amazing clarity. Let us consider, for example, certain aspects of Sophocles' *Oedipus the King.*

Unfortunately, the name of the tragic hero of the play has become associated in modern times with a neuropathic condition that bears no real relationship to the emotional disposition of Oedipus himself. It results from the strange accident that nineteenth-century psychologists were sufficiently well educated to draw names, when necessary, from classical literature.

Sophocles is retelling in dramatic form an old and legendary story—one that he knows, one that he expects his audience to know. What is significant, in view of the patriarchal nature of Greek society in Sophocles' days, is that he doesn't feel the need to explain it on the one hand or remotivate it on the other. We shall see that other writers, dealing with somewhat similar legends, felt the need to remotivate. If we accept an early matriarchate and a long subsequent period of transition, then it is clear that the real sovereign of Thebes, by virtue of maternal inheritance, is Jocasta. The claim of Oedipus to the exercise of sovereignty is solely that he becomes the husband of Jocasta (the fact of their relationship, of course, is unsuspected by all parties); he rules for her, for she is the real heir (heiress, if you prefer) of the kingdom.

But the traditional position of the brother, here represented by Creon, is not forgotten. Consider the following dialogue from the violent quarrel scene:

Creon: Answer me then. Are you not married to my sister?
Oedipus: That cannot be denied.
Creon: And do you not rule as she does? And with a like power?
Oedipus: I yield her all she asks for.
Creon: And am I not the equal of you both?

And after the self-imposed blindness and abasement of Oedipus, it is Creon who rules Thebes. This is, in fact, a reasonably perfect picture of a pre-patriarchal state in the Transistion Period; it gives the play a rationale it would not otherwise have.

Similar allusions to such a Transition Period are numerous in Greek literature and legend. Let us consider for a moment the Homeric epics.

If we concede inheritance through the maternal line, and therefore legal possession in the female, we not only enhance the behavior of Penelope through the long period of Odysseus' absence and presumed death, but also we elevate Telemachus from a ninny into someone occupying an unfortunate but understandable position. That is, the suitors are now applying for a position of authority to which Telemachus would have no real claim in a matriarchy. After all, in the latter years of his mother's nocturnal unravelling, Telemachus was fully mature in terms of his own day, and even by our standards, about old enough to vote.

Furthermore, if the legal—and in those days that meant also the divine—right of inheritance lay in the maternal line, and if the husband automatically exercised authority in her name, then the seduction of Helen, her removal to Troy, and her subsequent marriage to a Trojan prince gave what would be even today a quasi-legal and at that time an actual justification to a Trojan claim of hegemony over her kingdom. Viewed in this light, the Trojan War becomes understandable as a Greek War of Independence. Helen becomes the symbol of sovereignty. Probably in her early sixties at the time, it is perhaps demeaning to reflect that not her face but her inheritance may have launched a thousand ships.[1]

There are still other examples that come readily to mind. It would be impossible to examine all of them, but we may recall that Admetus ruled ancient Thessaly, not in his own inherited right, but because he was the husband of Alcestis. And notice too that as ancient stories pass through a shadow zone—a Transition Period between a matriarchy and a true patriarchy—incidents inherent in the story, incidents that would be self-sufficing in one tradition, must be modified and welded onto new material in order to satisfy a newer tradition.

Thus, in the fabled royal lineage of "marble Athens," Xuthus rules because he is the husband of Creusa, and it is the wife Creusa who has inherited the kingdom. So far this fits in naturally with our concept of a Transition Period between a matriarchy and a patriarchy. However, the demands of a mixed tradition require a son as the next inheritor of the kingdom. In the story as we have it, this demand is filled by the person of Ion, who later becomes King of Athens. (In some earlier and more primitive genealogy, incidentally, Ion may not have been a son at all.) But even here the vestiges of an old matriarchate remain; for this Ion is not the issue of Creusa and Xuthus, but of Creusa and a father unknown. As is not unusual in such ancient stories which must supply a paternity for someone for whom in his own time there would have been neither interest in nor question of paternity, a god is conveniently substituted. Thus Ion is said to be the son of Apollo. Remember that Helen of Trojan fame is established through her mother Leda; paternity in her case is ascribed to Zeus himself.

Another interesting point, where Ion is concerned, is that Xuthus, on the advice of and through the divine intercession of the Delphic god, selects Ion as his successor. This is interesting because there are other examples in the Transition Period where the wife's husband is instrumental in determining the succession. So long as he selects one of the daughters of his wife (or bestows his blessing on a traditionally accepted daughter), the system of matriarchy continues, though in this modified form that I call the Transition Period. It is only when, in violation of ancient practice, he selects a son, and his own son specifically, that the system of matriarchy gives way to the beginnings of a true patriarchy.

But I spoke of the husband bestowing his blessing on a particular daughter as successor to her mother. And this is the real opening wedge to a patriarchy, for what it amounts to is this: the father selects a husband for his daughter and then trains him to rule for the new queen as he has ruled for his own wife. At this point, of course, he has completely replaced the uncle in the social system.

All of us are familiar with the Continental Celtic and Germanic fairy-tales; they are veritable store-houses of residuals. A persistent characteristic of them is that the "Prince," who, though of royal family, has no kingdom of course, attains a kingdom by marrying a "Princess," (usually, by the way, the youngest daughter of a reigning family); and he is generally selected by the girl's father, who has set for the one or several suitors some difficult or nearly impossible task.

This is a persistent theme, even when reduced to a substratum, in all the early literature and fabled history of Western Man. To return to the ancients, Hippomenes gains a kingdom by marrying Atalanta. And, in the fables of the Romans, Aeneas is twice in the position of kingly power: once by a temporary liaison with Dido of Carthage; later by a permanent marriage with Lavinia. And note that the city they founded bore the name Lavinium.

But far more interesting to us than Ion, King of Athens, is Arthur, King of Briton. As we have the story from Malory — and through Malory from his own sources — Arthur, himself the Pendragon in his maturity, is the son of Uther Pendragon. But the story of Arthur, as we all know, is a very ancient one; and, very clearly, in its original form there was a greater need for Arthur to be the son of Igraine (the mother) than of Uther (the father). The account of Arthur's conception and paternity, as it has come down to us through medieval sources, represents that strange welding of new material onto an old stock to meet the needs of a later demand for patriarchal inheritance.

Briefly, Uther is at war with the Duke of Tintagel largely because of his love for Dame Igraine, the Duke's wife. Through the machinations of Merlin—that strange and wondrous mixture of Druid magician and Christian priest—Uther is magically transformed into the physical likeness of the Duke, spends the night with Igraine, and begets Arthur.

And even as in the classical story of Xuthus and Ion, the father designates his successor. Arthur, like Ion, is reared away from his parents and is unaware of his lineage. Merlin, now cast in the role of oracle, comes to Uther as that king lies dying, and, in the presence of the barons assembled, asks whether Arthur shall be King and Pendragon after Uther's days. And Uther, giving the child his own blessings and praying God's for him as well, yields up the ghost.

But the Arthurian cycle, complex enough in itself, is made infinitely more complicated by the infusion of the great adventure of the Grail; and in one of the branches of this complex matter, as Jessie Weston pointed out, it is not Perceval, but Gawain, who . . .

> . . . is far more closely connected with the Arthurian legend, occupying, as he does, the traditional position of nephew, Sister's Son, to the monarch who is the centre of the cycle; even as Cuchullinn is sister's son to Conchobar, Diarmid to Finn, Tristan to Mark, and Roland to Charlemagne. In fact this relationship was so obviously required by tradition that we find Perceval figuring now as sister's son to Arthur, now to the Grail King, according as the Arthurian, or the Grail, tradition dominates the story.[2]

Just two more examples need be cited to show how widespread and lasting in the literature of the West was the shadow cast by an ancient matriarchy and its subsequent Transition Period.

If you will accept for a moment one definition of tragedy, especially primitive tragedy (and I do not use the word *primitive* in any pejorative sense), as a dramatic spectacle wherein a representative man, generally of exaggerated stature, rebels against the moral order only to be destroyed by it, then we may bring together several fragments of the pattern we have been examining into a unified field of focus. Let us assume an ancient story-radical within the "moral order" of a late Transition Period, one in which inheritance is not only through the maternal line but specifically through the youngest daughter, as I believe it to have been generally among the Celtic tribes.

Let us assume as well that authority is exercised by the husband and that it is his duty within this moral order to recognize the husband of the youngest daughter as the inheritor of that authority and, concomitantly, to train him for it. Then, within this moral order, if the father recognizes instead the husband of any other daughter as his own successor, he has violated that moral order. It does not matter within this framework what his reasons are—they may seem to him good and sufficient at the time, or he may even be innocent of intent to violate the moral order (as in the case of Oedipus)—his very act alone precipitates the tragedy. Expressed thus baldly, the root of the tale lacks savor; yet the story in just this form would be at once satisfying and cathartic to an audience living within such a moral order. Centuries, or a millenium, later the story would require new motivation, a motivation within the Christian moral order. The new motivation, if the father is to become both the catalyst of tragedy and its victim, must concern itself with the *reason* for the father's action; and no more potent reason could suggest itself in violation of the Christian order than pride—senile pride, if you will. And this, of course, is precisely the new motivation that the story has when we meet it as Shakespeare's *King Lear.*

Part of what we have been discussing may explain the two marriages, and the later necessity for remotivating one of them, in the *Hamlet* story; for this, too, clearly descends from an ancient story-radical. In the matriarchal tradition, the inheritance of the kingdom was through Gertrude; accordingly, her two marriages, one to Hamlet *père,* the other to Claudius, are absolutely essential to the plot itself. But in a later patriarchy, the second marriage is no longer essential and consequently has to be remotivated.

Notes

[1]Helen's "divine" and "natural" rights to the throne are further emphasized by the fact that her natural descent is through her mortal mother; her divine right is that she is the daughter of Zeus.

[2]Jessie L. Weston, *From Ritual to Romance,* (Doubleday Anchor Books), Doubleday and Company, Inc., New York, 1957. P. 191 f.

About The Authors

Hazel Sullivan, A.B., M.A., is a member of the Evening Division Faculty of the University of Miami, where she teaches classes in fiction writing. Her articles on writing techniques have appeared in *The Writer* and *The Writer's Handbook.*

Natalie Grimes Lawrence, A.B., M.A., is Professor of English and Humanities at the University of Miami. She is the author of a number of studies in Shakespeare and other Renaissance dramatists.

William L. Halstead, B.A., M.A., Ph.D., is Professor of English and a member of the Graduate Faculty in the University of Miami. He is a recent contributor to the *Readers Companion to World Literature,* Dryden Press and Mentor Books.

John I. McCollum, Jr., B.A., M.A., Ph.D., is Associate Professor and Chairman of the Department of English in the University of Miami. He has contributed to the bibliographical studies of the Modern Humanities Research Association and is the editor of *The Age of Elizabeth* and *The Restoration Stage.*

J. A. Reynolds, B.A., M.A., Ph.D., is a member of the Graduate Faculty and Professor of Medieval Language and Literature in the Department of English at the University of Miami. He is the author of *Heraldry and You,* Thomas Nelson & Sons, New York.